# COLORWASH
# BARGELLO QUILTS

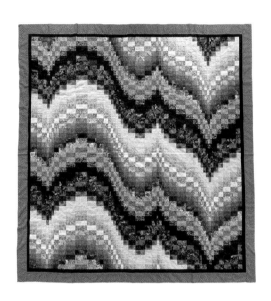

# COLORWASH BARGELLO QUILTS

## BETH ANN WILLIAMS

### *Martingale*™
### & COMPANY

WOODINVILLE, WASHINGTON

## CREDITS

President ⌒ Nancy J. Martin

CEO ⌒ Daniel J. Martin

Publisher ⌒ Jane Hamada

Editorial Director ⌒ Mary V. Green

Editorial Project Manager ⌒ Tina Cook

Technical Editor ⌒ Toni Toomey

Copy Editor ⌒ Ellen Balstad

Design and Production Manager ⌒ Stan Green

Illustrator ⌒ Laurel Strand

Photographer ⌒ Brent Kane

Cover & Text Designer ⌒ Stan Green

That Patchwork Place® is an imprint of
Martingale & Company™.

Colorwash Bargello Quilts
© 2001 by Beth Ann Williams

Martingale & Company
20205 144th Avenue NE
Woodinville, WA 98072-8478 USA
www.martingale-pub.com

Printed in the USA.

06 05 04 03 02 01    8 7 6 5 4 3 2 1

**Library of Congress Cataloging-in-Publication Data**

Williams, Beth Ann.
    Colorwash bargello quilts / Beth Ann Williams.
        p. cm.
    ISBN 1-56477-355-8
        1. Patchwork—Patterns. 2. Strip quilting—Patterns.
        3. Patchwork quilts. I. Title.

TT835.W5348 2001
746.46'041—dc21                                    00-065360

## MISSION STATEMENT

We are dedicated to providing quality products and service by working together to inspire creativity and to enrich the lives we touch.

# DEDICATION

To my amazing husband, John, and to our wonderful daughters,
Caryl Elisabeth and Connor Marie, for sharing this incredible journey with me.

# ACKNOWLEDGMENTS

My deepest thanks to:

Our parents, J. E. and Sue Williams and Dr. James King and Carol Brennan King;

Our family and friends, especially Amy Logsdon, Barbara Hulet, Diane Peffer, Cindy Rowe, Mary Taylor, and Kathi Wallace, who have encouraged us, comforted us, and rejoiced with us at various points during the last year;

Sue and Michael Callihan for their continuing friendship, artistic inspiration, and companionship on our mutual spiritual, physical, and emotional journeys;

Roxann Shier, Nancy Glazier, and Connie Young, who are always ready to step in and help out in very practical ways, from rides to kid care to meals—you guys are life support!

The team at Grand Quilt Co. in Comstock Park, Michigan: Lori and Verlyn Verbrugge, Sarah Verbrugge, Adrienne Alexander, Karen Beaman, Linda Chmielewski, Pam Crans, Estella Fessenden, Dolly Lehman, Jane Levering, Ginger Hoop, Meghan Hoop, Caitlin Hoop, Nancy Roelfsma, and Dawn Ysseldyke for their generosity, helpfulness, encouragement, and friendship through all the many stages of our lives—personally as well as professionally;

Gay Bomers of Sentimental Stitches, who was very helpful to me in discussing (and hunting for photographs and documentation!) the relationship of modern bargello quilts to more traditional quilt patterns.

Cathy Babbidge, who pieced "Aurora" in the middle of selling her house and packing to move;

Pam Crans, who not only pieced "Cascade" but also helped gather all the necessary release forms, pick up quilts, and generally make life a lot easier for me!

Terrie Wicks, who without much advance notice, agreed to quilt "Aurora" and "Monet's Garden" and did a wonderful job;

Amy Logsdon, Barbara Williams Hulet, Diane Peffer, and Bobbie Pillow, who generously agreed to lend me their quilts during the months of photography and production;

My mother-in-law, Sue Williams, who picked out and purchased untold yards of beautiful fabric for me. You have a wonderful eye, Mom!

Toni Toomey, who really caught my vision for this book and whose encourgement, creative thinking, and constant feedback have been of tremendous value to me;

All my students for their creativity and enthusiasm—you always inspire me.

# CONTENTS

# INTRODUCTION

Discussions of bargello quilts usually lead to the subject of bargello needlepoint. Often called Hungarian point, flame stitch, or Florentine work, this centuries-old needle art differs from bargello quilting in many ways, but there are important characteristics that link traditional bargello needlepoint with contemporary bargello quilt piecing. Exciting and often illusionary effects are achieved primarily through the use of color and/or value, colors are often shaded from light to dark or vice versa, and rows of color follow the same pattern once the basic design line is established. There are, of course, notable exceptions, but the basic concepts remain constant.

Bargello needlepoint is not the only precursor to bargello quilts. Although assembled perhaps in different ways, vintage Postage Stamp, Sunshine and Shadow, and Trip Around the World quilts often bear a strong resemblance to contemporary bargello quilts, both in scale and in color usage. Many incorporate distinct gradations in color and value, as do many traditional Blazing Star, Radiant Star, Lone Star, and Star of Bethlehem quilts. In the current quilt revival, Alison Goss was a trailblazer in introducing and popularizing bargello techniques in the quilt world. Other notable names include Diane Wold, Marilyn Doheny, and Marge Edie, all of whom have written wonderful books on bargello piecing.

There's no doubt that modern strip-piecing methods pioneered in the 1970s by innovative quiltmakers such as Barbara Johannah were instrumental in the technical development of bargello quilts. Certainly the availability of such tools as rotary cutters, mats, and large (accurate!) acrylic rulers has revolutionized quiltmaking and made bargello piecing possible, even for the fainthearted among us.

Some bargello designs—needlepoint or quilt—have well-defined divisions of color and contrasting values. However, the bargello designs in this book emphasize blending colors and visual textures of fabrics to create smooth transitions or "washes" of color across the face of the quilt. This approach is very similar to the popular watercolor concept in quilting, as described by Pat Maixner Magaret and Donna Slusser in their books, *Watercolor Quilts* (That Patchwork Place, 1994) and *Watercolor Impressions* (That Patchwork Place, 1995). The main difference is that my bargello quilts have an increased emphasis on color and color harmonies, as well as on value and visual texture. Deirdre Amsden's book, *Colorwash Quilts: A Personal Approach to Design and Technique* (That Patchwork Place, 1994), provided my initial introduction to colorwash/watercolor quilts. Seeing Deirdre's work for the first time was one of the great "Aha!" moments in my quilting career.

Each of us has our own ideas about which techniques are the most successful (or easiest to sew) and what kinds of fabric combinations we find most appealing. It is not my intention to imply that the methods in this book are the last word on how to make bargello quilts. Instead, it is my desire to share what I have found that works best for me and to encourage others to make use of the information that is helpful to them while feeling perfectly free to make innovations of their own along the way. Keep me posted on what works for you!

# EQUIPMENT AND SUPPLIES

## FABRIC

Good-quality, colorfast, 100 percent–cotton fabric is the best choice for these projects. It holds its shape when pressed, washes easily, and ages gracefully. While I do use some subtle prints and tone-on-tone fabrics that give the appearance of being solid when viewed from a distance, I very rarely use solid-color fabrics for bargello quilts. I find fabrics with visual texture to be much more interesting and easier to blend. However, this is a personal preference, not a hard-and-fast rule. Don't feel that you need to copy the colors and prints that I have used; use colors and fabrics you like! The sections on "Selecting a Palette" on page 15 and "Creating Colorwash Effects" on page 21, respectively, are designed to assist you in selecting the fabrics for your quilt.

When selecting fabrics for a bargello project, try to stick with fabrics that are similar in weight or tightness of weave. Mixing loosely woven fabrics with tightly woven fabrics invites inconsistencies into your piecing; the loosely woven fabrics tend to stretch more than the other fabrics and/or become distorted during the construction process. Loosely woven fabrics also tend to shrink more when washed,

often shrinking more in one direction than another, which provides a good argument for washing fabric before using it. I also recommend washing your fabrics before you use them to remove any sizing, finishes, or excess dye. Be particularly careful with deep red and violet fabrics. They are the most likely to bleed, although I rarely have problems. When there is a problem, however, it can be huge, so it pays to be careful! If necessary, press the laundered fabric to remove any wrinkles.

## SEWING MACHINE AND ATTACHMENTS

### SEWING MACHINE

For piecing the quilt tops, you'll need a good straight stitch and a very consistent seam allowance, especially when sewing over multiple layers. If you elect to machine-quilt your bargello top, you may also need to know how to change the presser feet, increase or decrease the tension setting for the top thread, raise and lower (or cover) the feed dogs, and adjust the pressure on the presser foot.

If possible, sew with your machine in a cabinet, or use an extension table or commercial portable table such as the Sew-Steady table. Having a large, flat surface on which to work can be a significant help when trying to keep long lines of piecing straight and machine quilting a smooth process.

It is very important that you diligently maintain your sewing machine, keeping it oiled (if appropriate) and cleaned regularly. Lint and debris can build up very quickly, especially in the tension discs, around the presser bar and needle bar, under the needle plate, and around the bobbin area. Your machine will get quite a workout, so treat it kindly!

> ## TIP:
> I use Synthrapol in the wash water if I am concerned about color bleeding. Synthrapol is designed to both remove excess dye and prevent it from redepositing on your other fabrics. It is available from quilt suppliers (see "Resources" on page 95).

> **TIP:**
> Stop and clean out your machine at least every six hours of continuous sewing. You'll be amazed at the improvement in stitch quality, tension control, and smoothness of operation.

If possible, use the walking foot made especially for your machine. If you cannot find your brand, try a generic walking foot. There are several different styles of generic walking feet; you may have to try more than one before you find a happy fit. Make sure that the *feeders* (also called *teeth* or *grippers*) inside the foot align exactly with the feed dogs on your sewing machine. If they do not, the fabric will not feed evenly, and you may be worse off than if you had no walking foot at all!

### QUARTER-INCH FOOT

Depending on the make and model of your machine, you may be able to choose from one or more different types of presser feet designed specifically to help you achieve perfect ¼" seam allowances. In some cases, the edge of the foot serves as a guide; in others, there is an  actual blade against which the fabric is guided as it is fed under the presser foot. Many people find a quarter-inch foot to be invaluable for constructing strip sets with consistently accurate seam allowances.

### WALKING FOOT/EVEN-FEED FOOT/ PLAID MATCHER

The walking foot/even-feed foot/plaid matcher attachment comes under a variety of guises. Not only does it have several different names, but also its appearance can vary widely. A walking foot is 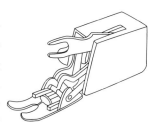 unique in that it allows multiple layers of fabric, such as an entire quilt "sandwich" (quilt top, batting, and backing) to move through the machine at an even rate, minimizing shifting. It does this by reproducing the action of the feed dogs below on the top layer (or layers) of fabric. This foot is indispensable for machine-guided machine quilting.

### DARNING/FREE-MOTION/ SPRING EMBROIDERY FOOT

The darning/free-motion/spring embroidery foot is yet another foot that not only goes by a variety of names, but can also vary quite dramatically in appearance from one brand to another. This special foot gives you the ability to move the fabric freely from side to side and front to back as 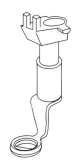 you sew. The foot itself moves up and down with the needle. When the needle is up, you can steer the fabric in any direction. When the needle is down, the foot descends to hold the fabric firmly against the machine's throat plate so that you do not end up with skipped stitches. This foot is indispensable for free-motion machine quilting.

As with the walking foot, it is best to use a foot made especially for your machine. If you cannot find your brand, there are several different styles of generic darning feet. You may need to try more than one.

# SEWING-MACHINE NEEDLES

Today there are several types of specialty needles available that make your sewing life much easier and help ensure high-quality results. Needles have two numbers, such as 60/8. The first number is the European size and the second number is the American size. European needles are sized according to the diameter (measured in hundredths of a millimeter from 60 to 120) of the steel wire from which the needle was made. The American size designations range from 8 to 21. The needle sizes used most often in quiltmaking are as follows: 60/8, 70/10, 75/11, 80/12, and 90/14. Unlike thread, which gets smaller in diameter as the weight number increases, needles get larger as the size number increases.

Needles also vary in terms of the shape of the point, the size and shape of the eye, and the contours of the needle shaft. The point, eye, and contours of each type of needle are engineered to work best with particular fabrics and threads. I have listed below the types and sizes of needles I find most helpful for the techniques in this book. I use the Schmetz versions of these sewing-machine needles.

Remember that fresh needles are important! Please don't wait until your needle breaks before you change it. Tufts of batting poking through the quilt, skipped stitches, or an odd popping sound when the needle hits the fabric are all signs that it is time for a new needle.

## MICROTEX SHARPS

Microtex Sharp needles have a very sharp point and narrow eye. I like to use size 70 for machine piecing, especially when using tightly woven fabrics such as high-quality batiks, since the needle makes such a lovely small hole and very straight stitches. The size 70 Microtex Sharp is also one of my favorite choices for machine quilting with nylon monofilament thread, although it is not as strong as the quilting needles and therefore a bit more subject to breakage. If you can find one in a small-enough size, a jeans or topstitching needle is an acceptable substitute.

## QUILTING NEEDLES

Quilting needles were developed specifically for quilting and have a strong shaft and sharp, tapered point. I often use a size 75 quilting needle for piecing. It is also one of my top choices for machine quilting with .004 nylon monofilament, 60-weight mercerized cotton thread, or 40-weight rayon thread. I reserve the size 90 for machine quilting with 30- to 40-weight mercerized cotton thread or 30- to 35-weight rayon thread.

## EMBROIDERY NEEDLES

Embroidery needles were designed to handle machine embroidery and decorative stitching. The eye is large and the scarf, which is the indentation behind the eye, is modified to reduce friction on threads that otherwise may have a tendency to fray or split. This is my favorite needle for machine quilting with rayon thread. I like to use sizes 75 or 90, with the size depending on the weight of the thread.

# THREAD

For piecing, use good-quality sewing thread (I prefer 50-weight mercerized cotton) in two neutral colors (one for the top thread, one for the bobbin thread) that blend with the fabrics you have selected for a given project.

For quilting, you can choose from nylon monofilament, mercerized cotton, or rayon decorative threads. While I tend to use a wide range of thread types and sizes in my work, I have a few favorites for my quilting top thread.

## NYLON MONOFILAMENT

For some machine-quilting techniques, you might wish to use nylon monofilament thread—always size .004—in either clear (for light fabrics) or smoke (for dark fabrics). The thread should be very fine, soft, and stretchy—nothing like the old "fishing line" invisible thread still found in some stores. Nylon monofilament thread sinks into the batting, especially after the quilt is washed, to give nice texture without adding color.

## MERCERIZED COTTON

I most often use 50-weight 3-ply, or 60-weight 2-ply mercerized cotton. These cotton threads are treated for strength and additional sheen that adds a subtle glow as well as color to the quilt.

Slightly heavier and therefore stronger 30- to 40-weight threads are also good choices for machine quilting, particularly when not quilting as heavily as I do in most of my quilts. When using 30- to 40-

weight machine-quilting thread in the top of your machine, you should generally use a similar weight and type of thread in the bobbin.

## RAYON

When choosing among the different weights of decorative rayon threads, I frequently select a 40-weight rayon, often in variegated colors. (Check the edge or the bottom of the spool to find the thread weight.) Rayon is great for adding rich color; variegated rayon adds even more interest, creating highlights as it changes in value.

You can also use metallic thread, but it requires specific techniques that I cannot cover in the scope of this book. Refer to *Machine Quilting with Decorative Threads* by Maurine Noble and Elizabeth Hendricks (That Patchwork Place, 1998) for detailed instructions on working with metallic threads.

NOTE: *Do not use nylon monofilament or rayon thread in your bobbin. With any of the threads just mentioned, I usually use 50- or 60-weight mercerized cotton in the bobbin and choose colors that blend with my bargello fabrics and/or my backing fabrics.*

# ROTARY-CUTTING EQUIPMENT

## ROTARY CUTTER

A rotary cutter with a sharp blade makes it much easier to cut straight, even strips with nice clean edges. Replace your blade often and you will be amazed at how much easier it is to use!

## CUTTING MAT

I recommend a gridded cutting mat at least 24" x 36" (the printed grid may be 23" x 35") in size. These mats can be expensive, but they seem to go on sale regularly; it is not unusual to find one at 30 to 50 percent off. Ask at your local sewing or quilting store, or check the many catalogs that cater to quilters.

## ACRYLIC RULER

Your acrylic ruler should be at least 24" long; a 6" x 24" ruler is ideal. Make sure that the lines on your ruler and the grid lines on your mat line up exactly, as sometimes there are slight variations between brands. My favorite rulers have both black and yellow markings, making them easily visible on both light and dark fabrics.

# PRESSING ESSENTIALS

## IRON

A good, clean steam iron is often helpful when blocking finished quilt projects, although it is unnecessary to use steam when pressing the strip sets or bargello segments.

## IRONING SURFACE

A pressing surface larger than the typical ironing board is helpful. Try a Teflon-backed pressing blanket, or improvise by layering cotton flannel sheets and/or old cotton towels over thick corrugated cardboard. (The latter protects your table from heat and/or steam damage.)

# DESIGN WALL

Although a vertical design wall is not mandatory, it is very helpful (and exciting!) to be able to look straight-on at the emerging design as you open up the looped bargello segments and lay them out next to each other.

If a permanent design wall is unavailable or impractical for you, you might consider purchasing one or more large pieces of foam-core board (or other lightweight, sturdy material) and covering them with flannel, cotton batting, or one of the new products sold especially for this purpose.

Another popular solution is to use the flannel side of a flannel-backed tablecloth as an inexpensive and very portable design wall. Use masking tape to tape it to a wall during use, and roll it afterward for easy storage.

# ASSORTED NOTIONS

## SCISSORS OR THREAD SNIPS

Thread snips or other small scissors are great to keep next to your sewing machine for clipping threads as you work.

## SEAM RIPPER

A seam ripper will be helpful when unpicking the seams to open up the looped bargello segments, as well as for any "sewing in reverse" that might be necessary along the way.

## SAFETY PINS

I like the medium (size 2 or 1½"-long) safety pins for pin-basting the quilt sandwich for machine quilting. Be sure to use pins that are sharp enough to penetrate the fabric easily. Never use old pins that show signs of rust or other residue; these can leave permanent stains on your quilt.

## STRAIGHT PINS

I like the long, fine, flat flower-headed pins that you can press over without melting the tops or leaving marks on your fabric. The very fine shaft is particularly helpful when pinning tightly woven fabrics such as batiks, since thicker pins may leave a small hole. There are a number of different look-alike brands that vary quite a bit in thickness; my favorites are 55mm in diameter.

## VALUE FINDER OR RUBY BEHOLDER®

A value finder is a red filter, usually made either of acetate or acrylic. Viewing a selection of fabrics through the red filter visually cancels out the color, simplifying the process of determining the relative values of the fabrics. The Ruby Beholder is a handy tool with a value finder on one end and a 1½" window template on the other end. (See "Value" on page 24 for more information on using a value finder.)

## LOW-TACK MASKING TAPE

The method for bargello piecing described in this book requires you to label your work with low-tack masking tape. Be careful what kind of masking tape you use. By low-tack, I'm referring to the painter's tape sold in home-improvement stores for masking such things as window frames when painting a wall. The tape is specially formulated to come off easily when the job is done, leaving no residue. Avoid the very sticky masking tapes that are sometimes sold in craft and quilt shops. These may leave a sticky or oily residue on your fabric when the tape is removed. Before you use any tape on your fabric, please do a spot test first on some scrap fabric to make sure that it will remove cleanly.

If you do not wish to use masking tape to label your strips and bargello segments, you can pin paper labels to them instead. However, I find them much more awkward to work around.

# BATTING

I prefer a low-loft, 80/20-percent cotton-poly blend batting, but I also occasionally use good-quality, low-loft polyester that has been bonded or needle-punched to prevent bearding. Read the package to determine if a particular batting should be washed before it is used and to find out how densely it needs to be quilted. Compare for yourself, and use what you like!

# Selecting a Palette

## Finding Inspiration

Inspiration for my artwork comes from my own experiences and interests, such as music, art, and travel. My color palettes are often suggested by my love for the natural world. Among the projects in this book, you might recognize the shifting patterns of color and light at dawn or dusk, mountain mists and shadows, lush vegetation and rippling water, and even the African savannah. I am also enthralled by ancient illuminated manuscripts, glittering Byzantine mosaics, rich oriental rugs, and embroidered and embellished textiles from around the world. My quilts often grow out of an attempt to capture, explore, and remember a specific moment of interplay of color, light, and line.

So where do you begin? Fabric selection can be the most personal and creative aspect of any quilt project. For some people, it seems to be a very natural and perhaps meditative or joyful process. For others, it can be intimidating, almost overwhelming, to be confronted with bolts upon bolts of fabulous fabrics and no clear idea of how to get started. The following suggestions are intended to simplify the process. Remember—they are only suggestions; feel free to be as adventurous as you like. After all, the important thing is to end up with a quilt you love!

First, ask yourself some questions: What mood do I want to create? Do I want my quilt to be bold and dramatic? Modern and sophisticated? Soft and dreamy? Warm and soothing? Cool and calming? Where will the quilt be displayed? Is it important to me to complement or coordinate with existing artwork, wallpaper, rugs, soft furnishings, or something else in the room?

The answers to these questions will help you choose a *focus fabric* to use as the visual guide for the rest of your fabric selections. This focus fabric should have the same overall effects, such as its colors and visual texture, that you want in your quilt. Your focus fabric probably will not be the most noticeable fabric in the quilt. In fact, it's not even necessary that this fabric end up in the finished quilt!

> ## TIP:
> Although we are working with fabric as a starting point, you can also work from a favorite painting, photograph, landscape, or almost anything else that inspires you!

With the focus fabric as your starting point, you will select fabrics with colors and prints that combine well to achieve the overall colorwash effect that you want for your quilt. The smooth "washes" of color characteristic of these bargello quilts are made by arranging fabrics that blend into one another to create a visual effect unlike any of the individual fabrics. For example, a group of six or seven fabrics placed side by side may take on the appearance of a band that migrates from a dark, warm violet to a pale, cool violet. We call this group of fabrics a *run*.

To continue, a run of violets might be put next to a run made up of a few neutral fabrics to create a transition to the next run, such as a group of startling yellows. Neutral fabrics can be very helpful to soothe the eye and float the bands of color. They can also increase the impact of adjacent colors and visual textures.

Once the runs are chosen, as shown below, they are joined with others into strip sets, which are the foundation of a bargello quilt. In the section "Visual Vocabulary" on pages 22–28, you will learn how to use color, value, and visual texture to create the desired effects of your runs.

Finally, whatever mood or style you choose for your focus fabric, sooner or later you will need to settle on a dominant fabric that will mark the visual movement of the design line across the quilt. This dominant fabric is usually the first color people notice when they look at the quilt. As a rule, the dominant fabric should be the darkest, warmest, and/or brightest fabric in the bargello portion of the quilt. Most often, this fabric is also the one you will use to follow the design line graphed in the project instructions for each quilt.

Sample Runs: These runs blend smoothly from one fabric to the next.

TIP:
**TIP:**
I find that fabrics with at least three to five distinct hues and/or values are generally the easiest to blend. The most likely exceptions to this rule may be the lightest light values and the darkest dark values in your strip sets.

1. Using the focus fabric as a guide, pull out fabrics from your stash (or store shelves) that match each of the colors and values in that fabric. Later, you will refine your fabric selection so the colors and values are in proportion with the colors and values in the focus fabric. For example, if there is a small amount of bright violet that acts as an accent in the focus fabric, your final fabric selections should include only a small number of bright violets. For now, however, begin by selecting any number of fabrics that catch your eye. These fabrics make up your basic palette.

# Building a Palette around a Focus Fabric

Generally, the easiest focus fabric to work from is a medium- to large-scale, asymmetrical, multicolored print containing a range of values from dark to light.

**TIP:**
Don't fall into the trap of overmatching the exact colors in your focus fabric; at this stage, minor variations in color, value, or intensity only add to the richness of your palette.

Easy-to-use focus fabrics combine several colors and a range of values.

2. Add fabrics that are noticeably lighter, darker, brighter, duller, and so on, than the fabrics you have already selected. This is your extended palette.

> ## TIP:
> Don't be afraid to add colors or values not found in your focus fabric. A color wheel may be helpful in suggesting exciting combinations; see "Color Harmonies" on pages 28–30 for more information.

3. Lay out the fabrics, each one overlapping the next. Expose about 2" of each one, creating runs as described on page 22. The runs do not need to be uniform in length. For example, in a project requiring a strip set of sixteen fabrics, you might have a gradated run of four blues, a run of six multicolor florals, a run of three violets, and a run of three neutrals.

# REFINING YOUR STRIP SETS

Once you have built your palette based on the focus fabric, begin to refine the order of your strip sets.

1. Using the number of fabrics listed in the project directions for the specific quilt you are making, arrange the runs to form a complete strip set. Most of the quilts in this book are made from strip sets composed of two to four runs. (You are free, however, to use more or fewer fabrics. You can also add or delete rows from the graphed design. Just keep in mind that any of these changes will affect the proportions of the quilt, final dimensions, and yardage requirements.)

Strip sets from "Enchanted Carpet," page 80, (top) and "Aurora," page 68, (bottom)

It is important that a strip set incorporates at least two areas that are darker than everything else and two areas that are lighter than everything else. One example of how this might work is to arrange the fabrics light to dark, dark to light, light to dark.

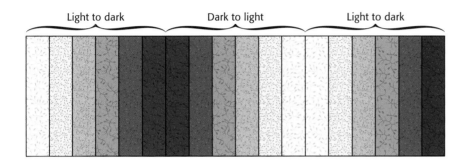

Another way might be to lay out the fabrics light to dark, light to dark.

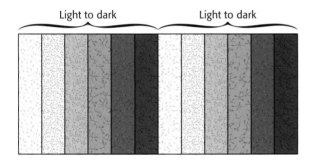

If the contrast between the very light fabric and the very dark fabric is too strong, you may wish to soften the contrast by inserting one or more medium values.

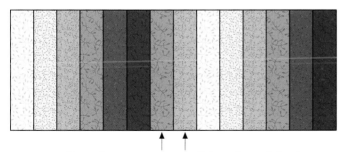

Use medium values to separate very light and very dark values.

I can't emphasize enough the importance of these value shifts for creating the effect of dynamic movement across the face of your bargello quilt.

TIP:
The last fabric in your strip set will end up immediately next to the first fabric because the strip sets are eventually sewn into tubes. Be sure that you like the combination!

2. Use a value finder or Ruby Beholder to check the blending and the movement of values (lights and darks) in your runs (see "Value" on pages 24–25).

3. Continue adding and eliminating fabrics until you have the number of fabrics indicated in the instructions for your quilt and are satisfied with your selection.

4. With about 2" of each fabric showing in the runs, make sure that the runs are arranged in the order you've planned for the strip sets. Compare the colors and values represented in the fabrics chosen for your strip set to the colors and values in the focus fabric to confirm that the proportions are the same. Double-check that you have areas of alternating values as discussed in step 1.

TIP:
If a favorite fabric stands out or "shouts" in a way that is disrupting to the flow of your strip set, you can usually balance it out by adding another fabric of equal value and/or color intensity in another part of the strip set.

5. Continue refining your fabric selections and their positions in the runs until you are satisfied with the results. Make note of the exact positions of the fabrics because you will number them in this order when you begin to assemble your strip sets.

6. Finally, identify the dominant fabric in your strip set. Keep in mind that it should generally be the warmest, brightest, or otherwise most noticeable fabric in the strip set. This is the fabric you will use to follow the project pattern.

TIP:
Although you may have one or more border fabrics in mind at this point, try not to make any final decisions until the main body of the quilt is complete. The fabrics interact with each other in surprising ways sometimes!

NOTE: *It is quite permissible to use the same fabric more than once in a strip set. In fact, you may want to repeat or reverse-repeat one or more runs. "Fire on the Savannah" on page 44, "After the Rains" on page 48, and "Aurora" on page 68 all use repeating runs. "Journey to Byzantium" on page 64 uses a reverse-repeat run.*

# CREATING COLORWASH EFFECTS

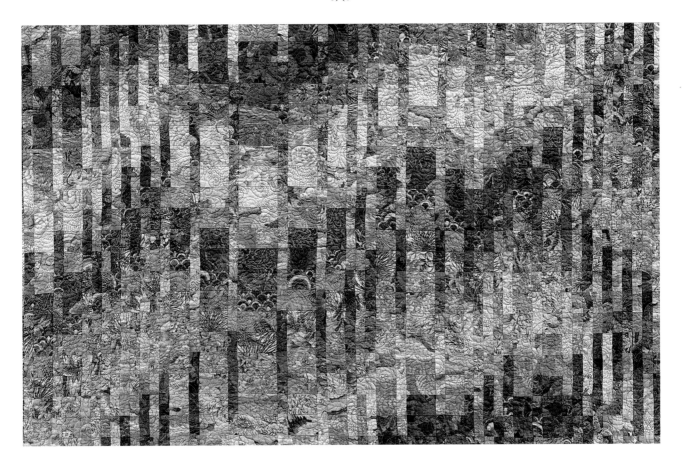

## COLOR, VALUE, AND VISUAL TEXTURE

If you are comfortable at this point with your ability to select a palette of fabrics and arrange runs and strip sets, go to "Constructing the Body of the Quilt" on page 31. However, if you would like more detailed information on how I assemble the fabrics for my quilts, this section is for you!

Color is probably one of the first things we notice about a particular quilt, but color is not absolute. Our perception of color is influenced by physiological, psychological, and emotional factors. And color is only one of three key factors that contribute to the visual effect of a run; value (the range from light to dark) and visual texture (created by the print in the fabric) are the other two factors.

I will explain how I use these three factors when creating smooth runs or washes of color for my bargello quilts, but don't be misled. Even though I describe them as distinct from each other, in reality two or more of these factors are usually working in concert to create the overall visual impact of a run. (See "Visual Vocabulary" on pages 22–28 for expanded descriptions of these factors.)

NOTE: *We each need to develop our own color sense, and just as importantly, the confidence to rely on our own intuition and experience.*

## CREATING RUNS BY COLOR

Runs of color may be one of the easiest ways to place fabrics next to each other. Multicolored print fabrics can be used to provide transitions between fabrics that are distinct in color. For example, a run of greens may be linked to a run of blues by placing print fabrics containing both green and blue between the two runs.

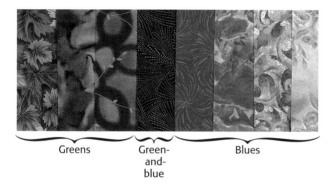

Greens  Green-and-blue  Blues

Neutral fabrics, such as cream and taupe, can also be used to make a transition from one color family to another. The photo below shows the transition from green to red-violet

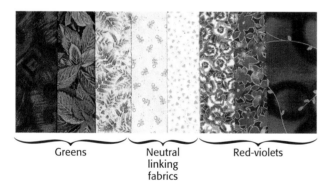

Greens  Neutral linking fabrics  Red-violets

## CREATING RUNS BY VALUE

Surprisingly, the real drama in your quilt will be achieved by the shifts in value that move through your runs. You accomplish gradations from light to dark (and vice versa) by arranging fabrics according to their values as well as their colors. When fabrics with similar values are grouped together, the effect is broad washes of color that create a pause in the rhythm of the design and bring your attention back to the colors in the quilt.

## CREATING RUNS BY VISUAL TEXTURE

Visual texture is often overlooked when selecting fabrics, yet it creates some of the most exciting color combinations. Fabrics with similar lines and shapes seem to blend into one another, even when they are different colors and/or values.

# HARMONY AND CONTRAST

Blending fabrics by their color, value, and visual texture is only part of the process of creating exciting color runs for a bargello quilt. You must also keep in mind the classic design principle that unity plus diversity equals harmony. I will discuss this principle more fully in the section "Visual Vocabulary" that follows, along with the concept of contrast. The color, value, and visual texture of your fabrics can be used to introduce contrast into your work while maintaining a cohesive whole. Variations in the scale of the fabric prints, sharp differences in value (light to dark), and strong shifts in color intensity (dull or bright) can be used to emphasize design lines or act as secondary accent lines that add interest to your bargello quilt.

# VISUAL VOCABULARY

Don't be discouraged if the following vocabulary words of the visual artist are unfamiliar. It's likely you already use some of these concepts intuitively when you make visual choices about fabrics. The following definitions may help you select fabrics when your eyes get stuck.

## COLOR AND HUE

We generally use the words *color* and *hue* interchangeably. In 1666, Sir Isaac Newton devised a system, which we call the color wheel, to illustrate important color relationships. Since then, other systems have been proposed by artists, scientists, physicians, psychologists, and even musicians; each system may differ slightly in the colors it includes, its primary colors, and the relationships between the colors. Each system is useful within particular disciplines and for specific purposes.

Currently, quilters can choose from two color systems—subtractive and additive—to identify their primary colors and the relationships between the colors. The subtractive system is based on the primary colors cyan (turquoise), magenta, and yellow. For selecting fabrics, I use the additive color wheel with the primary colors red, yellow, and blue; and the color relationships described by Swiss colorist Johannes Itten.

Itten positioned twelve colors equidistant on the color wheel. These colors could then be divided into three sets of colors. The first is the set of primary colors (red, yellow, and blue), which are pure hues not obtainable by mixing. Next is the set of secondary colors (orange, green, and violet) made by mixing two adjacent primaries. And finally, the set of tertiary colors (red-orange, yellow-orange, yellow-green, blue-green, blue-violet, and red-violet), which are made by mixing two adjacent hues—one primary and one secondary. All colors described in Itten's system have their origin in the pure hues of the color wheel.

> ## TIP:
> It is helpful to look at a print fabric from at least six feet away to determine its dominant color.

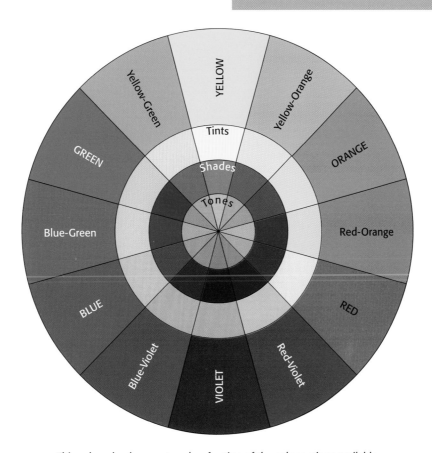

This color wheel presents only a fraction of the color options available.

## NEUTRALS

Neutral fabrics can unite, separate, or showcase colors, providing visual relief without altering the basic color relationships. "Autumn Glow" on page 60 uses neutrals to float bands of color. "Enchanted Carpet" on page 80 uses neutrals to float the medallion in the center of the bargello. The blues in "Cascade" on page 52 are clarified and emphasized along the creamy section running through the middle of the quilt, while in other areas they are allowed to overlap and blend with neighboring colors to create new combinations.

Black, white, and gray are the true neutrals. Quilters also consider beige as neutral, as well as pale (light-value) and dull (low-intensity) versions of other colors, such as soft browns, taupes, gray tints, and creams.

Examples of neutral fabrics

## VALUE

The word *value* describes the lightness or darkness of a color. Each color has a range of values, which can be compared to a gray scale that goes from white (highest value), through shades of gray (medium values), all the way to black (lowest value). Regardless of their colors, two or more fabrics that are close in value will appear to be the same shade of gray in a black-and-white photocopy. Looking through a Ruby Beholder (or other red value finder) is one way to judge the relative values of one or more fabrics, since it visually cancels out color. However, since the value finder is red itself, it is sometimes misleading. Red fabrics may appear lighter than they truly are, and green fabrics darker.

In a pinch, you can determine the relative values of two fabrics by placing them side by side and squinting at them. As you squint, the colors become less clear and their relative values emerge. When you view them this way, two fabrics that are very close in value become indistinguishable from each other.

The terms *shade* and *tint* are also related to value. Adding black to a pure hue creates a *shade*. A shade is always a darker value than the original color. The amount of black added to a color determines how dark or low in value the shade will be. For example, adding a small amount of black to pure red will make a slightly darker red or scarlet; increasing the amount of black can turn the red darker and darker, but the color is still red. Shades can be earthy or deep and mystical in feeling, depending on their visual warmth. (See photos of "Fire on the Savannah" on page 44 and "Enchanted Carpet" on page 80.)

Adding white to a pure hue creates a *tint*. A tint is always a lighter value than the original color. The amount of white added to a color determines how light or high in value the tint will be. For example, adding a small amount of white to pure red will make a slightly lighter red, which we usually call dark pink; increasing the amount of white can turn the red lighter and lighter to what we would call pale pink, but the color is still red. Tints create a cool, airy, and delicate mood. (See photo of "Monet's Garden" on page 56. Although it is certainly not based on tints alone, the many tints I used help define the overall feeling of the quilt.)

Value is often the predominant factor in defining an overall design. Value also can be used to establish contrast and depth. Visually, dark values tend to recede and light values to advance, although this tendency can be overridden if the dark fabric is very warm and/or intense.

Finally, value is relative; it is affected by the surrounding values. Often the same fabric can be used as a medium in one run or section of a strip set, and as a dark in another. In a traditional quilt, values may be placed in a consistent manner from block to block for a more formal approach, varied from block to block to introduce a feeling of spontaneity and unpredictability, or moved across the entire surface of the quilt to de-emphasize the underlying block structure (if any) in favor of an overall impression of light receding or advancing across the face of the quilt. Rearranging values can produce startlingly different effects within the same pattern. In a color-wash bargello quilt, we do not want to draw attention to all the little squares and rectangles we have sewn together. Instead, we are trying to create streams of color and light flowing across the surface of the quilt.

> **TIP:**
> Most people tend to buy fabrics in medium values; additional light lights and deep darks are often needed to create a "healthy" palette.

## INTENSITY, SATURATION, AND TONE

The term *intensity* refers to the strength or purity of a color. A color of pure intensity is *saturated*. Art created with pure colors tends to be dramatic and energetic, and has high visual impact. (See photo of "After the Rains" on page 48.) A color dulled by adding gray loses intensity and becomes a *tone*. The amount and value of gray added to a pure color will change its intensity along with its value. For example, a small amount of a medium-value gray may turn red into a dark rose, while a large amount of pale gray will turn red into a light dusky rose.

> **TIP:**
> To help you visualize the distinctions between tints, tones, and shades, remember these examples: pure color = red; tint (red + white) = pink; shade (red + black) = scarlet; tone (red + gray) = dusky rose.

Fabrics in various shades of gray are not very plentiful, nor would they look particularly pleasing in a color run. However, another way to create the effect of a color's tone is to use its color complement (directly opposite hue on the color wheel) in the adjacent fabric. Colorists know that a hue and its complement can be mixed to achieve a neutral "gray." Thus, instead of adding a gray made with black and white, colorists often mix a hue with its complement to create a rich tone of the pure hue.

As with value, the tone and intensity of color is relative. The fabrics surrounding a given fabric will always influence the way we perceive it. Fabrics that are low in intensity look muted or muddy. Grouping low-intensity fabrics next to one or more higher intensity fabrics helps the purer colors advance visually. "Aurora" on page 68 uses different runs of blue, some relatively clearer and more intense, and some that are much more toned down. This increases the sense of depth in the overall composition.

## VISUAL TEMPERATURE

Visual temperature refers to the relative warmth or coolness of a color. The warm colors on a color wheel are yellow through red; the cool colors are violet through green. However, since visual temperature is relative, warm and cool variations can also be found in all color families, regardless of position on the color wheel. A color family includes all the shades, tints, and tones of a pure hue. Even neutrals possess visual temperature.

When warm and cool colors are combined, warm colors generally advance and cool colors recede. Warm accents can add sparkle to a cool quilt; cool accents can soothe a warm quilt. "After the Rains" on page 48 is an example of a rather low-value and intensely saturated cool palette, with high-value warm accents. Intensity can also accentuate differences in visual temperature.

## VISUAL TEXTURE

Visual texture is a description of the way a fabric looks (not how it feels). The following design elements all contribute to visual texture and the sometimes-elusive quality of pattern character.

## Motif

A motif is the dominant design element, such as floral, geometric, dot, or conversation prints. Fabrics can be scenic, realistic, stylized, abstract, or geometric in style. (Please be aware that these labels are not all-inclusive!) Fabrics with similar motifs tend to blend into each other, despite differences in color, especially when they are also similar in value.

Fabrics with a variety of visual textures

## Ground Color

Ground color is the background color on which a motif is placed. Fabrics with similar ground colors can be placed next to each other to serve as transitional elements in achieving smooth changes in value and/or color.

Fabrics with similar ground colors

## Colorway

A colorway is the particular combination of colors used in a print fabric. Many fabrics are printed in multiple colorways. Using two colorways of the same fabric next to each other can sometimes create an easy shift from one color family to another.

Examples of different colorways

## Coverage

Coverage is the spacing of motifs on the fabric and may also be referred to as density. Using two or more fabrics with similar coverage can lead to a feeling of sameness among the fabrics. Grouping fabrics with similar coverage can also increase the illusion of wide bands of flowing color, de-emphasizing the characteristics of the individual fabrics.

## Layout

Layout is the manner in which the design elements are printed, such as random, one-way repeat, two-way repeat, and so on.

## Scale

Scale is the size of the motif in printed fabrics. Small-, medium-, and large-scale prints can be used in bargello to create different effects. In a bargello quilt, an overabundance of multicolored, small-scale prints in close proximity may seem overly busy and lose the overall movement of the design line, particularly when the fabrics are similar in value.

A variety of print scales

Tone-on-tone fabrics are small- to medium-scale subtle prints designed to function or read as solids when viewed from a distance. When combined with other scales, these fabrics can add a bit of visual texture and strong color interest without adding the potentially hard edge of a solid-colored fabric.

> ## TIP:
> Although most people find they have a preference in scale, using a variety of scales can help avoid monotony and enhance your quilt.

As an alternative to solid or tone-on-tone fabrics, I love to use mottled prints. While these prints are generally subtle or even indistinct, soft changes in value and/or color or intensity often give the impression of an internal glow. Mottled prints can be monochromatic or can combine two or more colors.

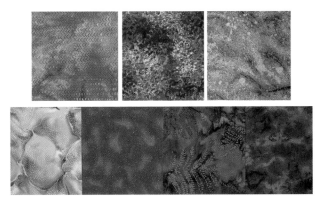

An assortment of mottled prints

Medium-scale prints are most people's favorite, probably because they are so versatile. They retain their design and color interest, even from a distance. They combine well with other scale sizes, usually without overpowering. But watch out—sometimes you can have too much of a good thing! Too many medium-scale prints can create an overblended effect, which can jeopardize the movement of the bargello design line. Medium-scale prints also tend to blend very well—especially when multicolored—so be sure to add enough contrast in hue and/or value to sustain the movement of color across the quilt. In "Journey to Byzantium" on page 64, several medium-scale prints are placed adjacent to each other, creating a wide wash of sparkling color and almost completely disguising the seam lines in some areas of the quilt.

Large-scale prints can add wonderful accents of unexpected colors and/or values to your color run as different portions of the print become visible in different areas of the quilt. Large-scale prints with high internal contrast can lead to lacy or sparkling areas within the design. "Mirage" on page 76 and "Enchanted Carpet" on page 80 both incorporate a number of large-scale prints with Asian motifs. "Cascade" on page 52 uses several medium- to large-scale florals. "Starry, Starry Night" on page 39 incorporates several mottled batiks that function as large-scale prints since the colors visible in each small rectangle cut from a single batik fabric may change completely from one piece to another. Depending on what small part of the fabric is visible, the results can be slightly unpredictable and sometimes even disconcerting; I also find it exciting.

> TIP:
> Moving a "window" template over a bolt of fabric can give you a preview of how it will look when you use it.

As with the other visual elements described, the scale of a fabric is relative and always affected by its neighbors. In practical terms, this does not mean you must use a large-scale print in every bargello quilt you make (although I generally do!) However, it does mean that you will probably be happier with your results if you try to use a variety of scales.

> TIP:
> Beware of the "pretty bolt" syndrome: what looks lovely on the bolts arranged on the cutting table next to each other may not look so wonderful when cut up in a quilt. It is important to have a combination of noisy and quiet fabrics to lead your eye around the surface of the quilt, balancing the design.

One strength (and weakness) of using fabric from one manufacturer's particular line is that the fabrics have been specifically designed to coordinate with each other. It is helpful to remember that a certain amount of contrast is an important element in creating a quilt that will be interesting to look at; too-little contrast can lead to visual mush and/or a very sedate and boring quilt. The scale of the design

motifs on the fabric as well as the color, value, and intensity should vary.

# COLOR HARMONIES

Colors affect each other in different ways. Combinations of colors can sparkle and energize, as they do in "After the Rains" on page 48, or calm and sooth as seen in "Autumn Glow" on page 60. For centuries, artists have used certain color combinations called *harmonies* to build the color schemes for their work.

Color harmonies are defined by the relationships of hues and their positions on the color wheel. For example, blue and its adjacent hues combine into one kind of harmony, while blue and the hue positioned opposite it on the color wheel make up a different harmony. These harmonies should not be regarded as rigid formulas but as inspirations to help you select colors that please you. In this section, I will introduce you to the most commonly used color harmonies, and share with you how they helped me create the color schemes for the quilts in this book.

Generally, I do not start with the color wheel or purposely select harmonies to use in quilts I am planning. However, I have found it to be an invaluable tool for analyzing the color relationships among the fabrics I select. The color wheel is also a wonderful guide for suggesting colors to remove when I want to simplify the palette. I also can use the color wheel to help me decide how to add colors, expand the palette, alter the color harmony, or choose one or more accent colors to spice things up.

## ACHROMATIC (WITHOUT COLOR)

The word *achromatic* means "without color." Neutrals such as white, black, and shades of gray make up an achromatic palette. Colors such as brown, gray-violet, beige, and cream also function as neutrals. An achromatic harmony is based on the exclusive use of neutral colors. Contrast (and therefore definition and interest) can only be achieved by manipulating values (light and dark) and the scale and styles of print patterns. Done well, an achromatic palette can yield a very sophisticated look.

## MONOCHROMATIC (ONE COLOR)

Monochromatic harmony is based on one color (hue) in a variety of tints, shades, and tones. Contrast may be introduced with variations in value and intensity. Neutrals can be added for extra interest without changing the overall color scheme of the quilt. "Star Kindler" on page 72 is essentially a monochromatic quilt, although it teeters on the edge of becoming analogous, a term that is explained in the next section.

## ANALOGOUS (ADJACENT COLORS)

On the color wheel, two to five adjacent colors are called *analogous*. Theoretically, analogous colors share a common source color. A five-color, side-by-side grouping may also be called an *extended analogous harmony*. "Cascade" on page 52 is based on an analogous color harmony of blue through red. Though less commonly used, a variation on the analogous color harmony may also be achieved by using every other hue from an analogous group on the color wheel.

## ANALOGOUS WITH AN ACCENT

An analogous harmony with an accent has three side-by-side colors with the complement (direct opposite on the color wheel) of one of the three used as an accent. Often this accent is the complement of the middle color of the three. "Starry, Starry Night" on page 39 uses an analogous grouping of blues and violets—with just a hint of teal—and a small amount of peachy pink as a complementary accent.

## EXTENDED ANALOGOUS WITH AN ACCENT

An extended analogous harmony with an accent has five side-by-side colors with the complement of one of the colors. The accent color is often (but not always) the complement of the middle color of the

five. In either case, adding a complementary, warm/cool contrast color as an accent can visually intensify the analogous colors. "Dreaming of the Ancient Ones" on page 41 shows an extended analogous palette with a complementary accent of yellow. Analogous harmonies tend to feel natural, peaceful, and balanced. Adding one or more accent colors (in small amounts) can enrich and deepen the palette.

## COMPLEMENTARY

Complementary color harmony is based on colors directly opposite each other on the color wheel. Except in the case of red and green, which can be used successfully in equal amounts, complementary colors are often paired in unequal amounts; the ratio is dependent on the relative intensity of the fabrics being used. Some basic ratios are red and green, 1:1; orange and blue, 1:2; yellow and violet, 1:3. Feel free, however, to vary the ratios to emphasize certain colors and/or values. Since complementary colors are often too strong when used together in their pure form, you may wish to tone down (lower the intensity of) one or both of the colors. "Aurora" on page 68 is an example of a complementary harmony based on blue and orange, with the orange softened to peach and a bit of violet acting as an accent color.

## SPLIT COMPLEMENTARY AND NEAR COMPLEMENTS

Another way to soften the contrast of complementary pairs is to use a split complementary harmony, which uses one complement and substitutes the other with the two colors on either side of the omitted complement. "Journey to Byzantium" on page 64 uses this harmony with red, orange, and blue-green. Alternatively, the omitted complement can be restored. The effect is similar to the "analogous with an accent" color harmony; the difference is one of emphasis. Using near complements, such as red and blue-green instead of red and green, can also provide a pleasing combination of colors. Neutrals can help separate and define complementary colors, as demonstrated in the wide expanses of white background on many traditional red-and-green (or rose-and-green) appliqué quilts.

## DOUBLE COMPLEMENTARY

A double complementary harmony uses two adjacent colors and their complements. "Island of the Blue Turtles" on page 42 is an example of this harmony, with yellow, yellow-orange, violet, and blue-violet.

## SPLIT DOUBLE COMPLEMENTARY

A split double complementary harmony uses two colors separated by a single color on the color wheel, and the complement of each color. For example, violet and yellow would be one pair of complements, and blue and orange would be the second pair of complements.

## TRIADIC

A triad is based on any three colors that are equidistant from one another on the color wheel. Red, blue, and yellow make up a triadic harmony. If this seems too bold, consider using their shades: burgundy, navy, and gold—classic! Adding the complement of one of the three colors as an accent can enrich the triadic harmony. "Fire on the Savannah" on page 44 is an example of a triadic harmony based on orange, green, and violet. "Autumn Glow" on page 60 and "Enchanted Carpet" on page 80 are also variations of triadic harmonies.

## TETRADIC

A tetrad is based on four colors equidistant from one another on the color wheel. Note that a tetradic harmony also uses two sets of complementary colors.

## POLYCHROMATIC

A polychromatic harmony uses many or all of the colors on the color wheel. (Most often, it involves either every color or every other color, all around the color wheel.) Rainbow harmony uses all twelve colors. One color may be chosen as dominant in order to unify a polychromatic color scheme. Although the warm golds visually dominate "Mirage" on page 76, this quilt actually uses every other color on the color wheel.

## COLOR PROPORTIONS

With any of the harmonies, keep in mind that the colors need not be used in equal proportions, values, or intensities. This is especially helpful when working with complementary harmonies. For example, adding a pure yellow fabric to a selection of violet fabrics might create a contrast that is too stark and distract from the unity of the quilt. On the other hand, incorporating a violet-print fabric that includes a bit of yellow might be just the warm accent an essentially violet quilt needs to make it sparkle.

Also, keep in mind that once you choose a specific color harmony, do not automatically exclude fabrics with colors not included in that particular harmony. The colors in the harmony you choose should be seen as the foundation of your color selections—not as members of an exclusive members-only club!

# CONSTRUCTING THE BODY OF THE QUILT

## CUTTING THE STRIPS

The bargello projects in this book may look complex, but they are actually fairly simple to construct. The key to success is completing each step with care.

Most projects begin with 2"-wide strips of fabric ("Aurora" and "Star Kindler" begin with 2½"-wide strips). The method I use for cutting strips in a short time requires you to pay close attention to the fabric grain and to carefully lay out and cut the fabric using the grid lines on your cutting mat and transparent ruler. But once you get the hang of it, you'll be able to cut out a whole quilt in no time at all.

1. Prewash all your fabrics and press, if needed, before cutting your strips.
2. On your cutting mat, fold your fabric in half, selvage to selvage. The selvages may not always line up perfectly, due to distortion during the production process. When you make the first fold, line up the fold with a grid line on your cutting mat. Try to fold the fabric along the grain line of the fabric. Don't be distracted by the print on the fabric. Most fabrics seem to be printed at least slightly off grain. Make sure the fabric lies smooth and flat, with no pulls or wrinkles along the fold. Even if the selvages are not exactly parallel to each other, it is more important that the fold is parallel to the fabric's threads.

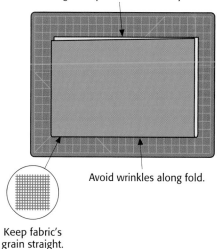

Selvages may not match exactly.

Avoid wrinkles along fold.

Keep fabric's grain straight.

3. Fold the fabric a second time so the first fold lines up roughly with the selvages. This second fold should follow the grain of the fabric and the grid lines on the cutting mat in the same way as the first fold.

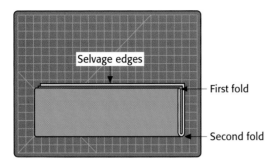

4. Trim the left edge (the right edge if you're left-handed) as shown in the illustration below, and cut the number of 2"-wide strips specified in the pattern. ("Aurora and "Star Kindler" call for 2½"-wide strips.) As you cut the strips, line up the ruler with the grid lines on the mat, also making sure that the fold lines are parallel with the grid lines. By keeping the fabric and the ruler lined up with the grid lines, you will get clean, straight edges on your fabric strips.

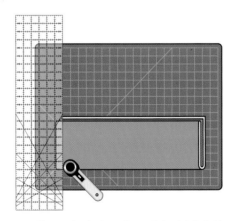

Line up both the ruler and the fabric fold with grid marks on the cutting mat.

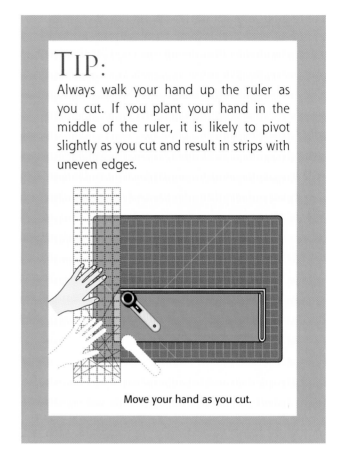

## TIP:

Always walk your hand up the ruler as you cut. If you plant your hand in the middle of the ruler, it is likely to pivot slightly as you cut and result in strips with uneven edges.

Move your hand as you cut.

# SEWING THE STRIP SETS

To keep the strips from becoming distorted while they're being sewn, join pairs of strips and then pairs of pairs. Also, as you press each pair of strips, be sure to press the seam allowances in the direction given in the project instructions.

1. Lay out your fabric strips in the order in which they will be sewn. Before you sew a strip, check the edges and use it only if its edges are very straight; avoid using strips that are crooked or bent.

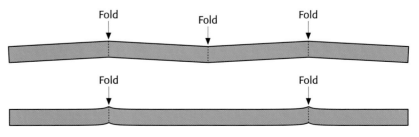

Don't use strips with crooked or uneven edges.

2. To avoid confusion, work on only one complete strip set or panel at a time. With small pieces of low-tack masking tape and a pen, label each strip with its correct sewing-order number. Avoid placing the tape in the seam allowance areas. When laying out the strips, line up the top selvage edges of the strips. The bottom edges may not all match due to variations in the widths of the original fabrics.

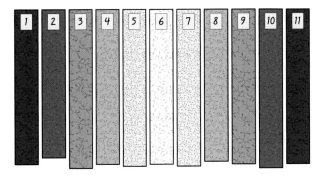

Number the strips.

3. Use a different thread color in the top than in the bobbin. Using a different thread color will come in handy later when you unpick a seam in each loop of bargello segments (see "Laying Out the Body of the Quilt" on page 35). Lining up the top edges of the strips, sew them into sets of two: Flip strip 2 on top of strip 1 so right sides are together; sew along the right-hand edge. Continue by sewing strip 4 on top of strip 3, and so on. Sewing the strips in pairs before joining all the strips together helps prevent the finished strip set from becoming bowed.

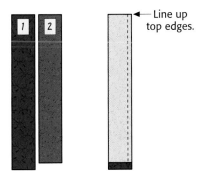

Line up top edges.

As you stitch the beginning and end of each seam, the fabric may have a tendency to slip to one side or another, distorting the first and last ½" of the seam.

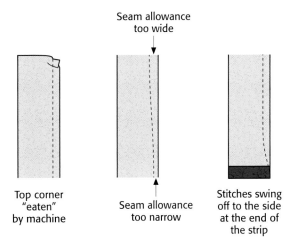

Top corner "eaten" by machine

Seam allowance too wide

Seam allowance too narrow

Stitches swing off to the side at the end of the strip

To avoid distortions at the beginning of a seam, I begin the seam line on a small scrap of fabric. Then I sew "on air" for a few stitches with the presser foot still down and begin the seam on the real fabric. I end the seam the same way, with a few stitches on air followed by a scrap piece of fabric or by the next pair of strips.

4. Press carefully. It's very important to lift the iron off the fabric as you move it along a seam. In other words, don't slide the iron along the fabric because this may stretch the seam slightly. To get a cleanly finished seam, press first from the back side to set the stitches.

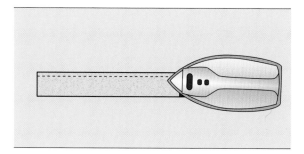

Press up and down. Don't slide iron.

Next, flip the piece over, right side up. Gently pull the strips apart with your fingers, making sure there are no tucks in the fabric as you press the seam to one side with the tip of your iron held at a slight sideways angle.

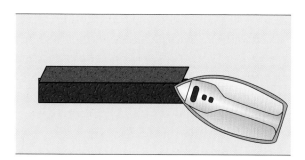

Press with tip of iron at a slight sideways angle.

Finally, press the piece once more from the right side, making sure the seam allowance is still pressed to one side. Note that each pattern indicates the direction in which the seam allowances of the strip sets should be pressed. Generally,

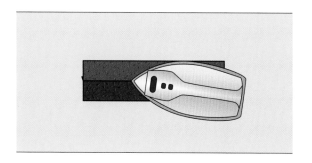

if you are making two strip sets, you will be directed to press the seam allowances of the first set toward the first strip and the seam allowances on the second set all toward the last strip. This pressing will allow the seam allowances to oppose each other and neatly butt against each other (or nest) when the individual bargello segments are sewn together.

5. Continue sewing the pairs of strips together, pressing after each round. Then sew and press the strip pairs. Be sure to sew the pairs in the same order that they are numbered. For example, flip pair 3 and 4 onto pair 1 and 2, and sew down the right edge. Continue joining the strips until the entire set is sewn into one panel or completed strip set.

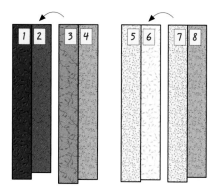

Sew strip pairs together.

Repeat steps 1 through 4 until your strip sets are completed.

# CUTTING THE BARGELLO SEGMENTS

Most of the projects in this book call for two strip sets. If you have followed the project instructions, you have pressed all of the seam allowances in one set toward the first strip in the set and in the other set toward the last strip. Now you will sew each strip set into a tube and cut loops according to the widths provided in the project instructions.

1. With right sides together, sew the top edge of the first strip to the bottom edge of the last strip in each of the strip sets to create tubes.

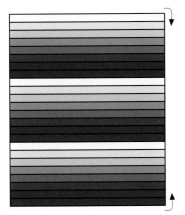

Sew the first and last strips together.

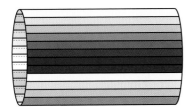

The strip set becomes a tube when the first and last fabrics in the strip set are joined.

2. Using the bargello segment-width charts provided for each project, cut loops (also known as bargello segments) from the tubes.

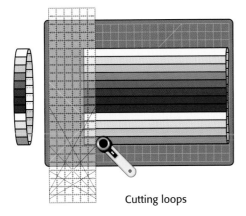

Cutting loops

Alternate the tubes as you cut, or cut all odd-numbered loops from the first tube and all even-numbered loops from the second tube. This will ensure that your seam allowances will oppose each other and make it much easier to assemble the quilt. On each loop, place a small piece of low-tack masking tape on the fabric you have chosen as the dominant fabric in your design. Write the segment number on the masking tape.

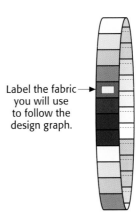

Label the fabric → you will use to follow the design graph.

# LAYING OUT THE BODY OF THE QUILT

Before you lay out the body of the quilt, you will need to open each loop to create bargello segments. At this point, the loops all look the same except for their widths. You will use the project design graph and the dominant fabric you've labeled to help you open the loops and watch the bargello design appear.

1. The design graph for each project shows the position of the dominant fabric in each segment. To determine where to open a loop, find the segment number on the design graph and count up from the dominant fabric to the top of the graph. On the loop, count the same number of pieces and unpick the seam in that spot.

TIP:
You can reuse the masking tape labels you used while sewing the strip sets together.

35

## TIP:
Unpicking seams will be much easier if you use a different color of thread in the bobbin than in the top. Clip the bobbin thread every three to five stitches, and you can usually pull the top thread out in one piece.

2. Move the low-tack masking tape labels to the top strips of the bargello segments (avoiding the seam allowances). These numbers can stay on until the entire bargello design has been completed. However, do try to avoid pressing directly on top of the tape with the iron when possible. Finally, make sure the seam allowances of the odd-numbered segments are pressed in the opposite direction from the seam allowances of the even-numbered segments.

3. If possible, lay out the bargello segments in order on a vertical design surface so you can check the emerging pattern against the project design graph as you proceed.

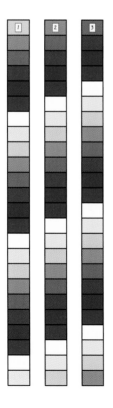

# ASSEMBLING THE BODY OF THE QUILT

As you did with the strip sets, sew the bargello segments together two by two, then four by four, and so on. Press carefully after each round of sewing. Continue until the entire design is completed. Because the seam allowances of odd-numbered and even-numbered segments were pressed in opposite directions, the seam allowances should butt against each other nicely, making it easy to match seams.

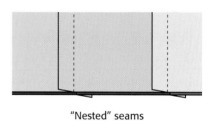

"Nested" seams

Remove the labels and admire your work-in-progress!

## TIP:
Try turning the quilt top upside down; you may find you like it better that way. The change can be amazing!

# ADDING BORDERS

Sometimes you may find that a bargello quilt is complete without a border, or you might feel that your quilt would look better with a narrower or wider border than I have suggested in the project directions. Follow your heart! No matter what your decision is, it is vital that you do not cut any border fabrics until the body of your quilt is complete. Variations in seam allowances, or even pressing, often affect the finished size of the bargello portion of a quilt top.

The yardage requirements for border fabric in this book assume that you will make butted (not mitered) borders, with outer borders cut on the lengthwise grain of the fabric for extra stability. (Unless I am using a striped border fabric that needs to be mitered for design reasons, I prefer to use butted borders with my bargello quilts.) Yardage requirements for narrow inner borders assume that the strips will be cut on the crosswise grain, from selvage to selvage.

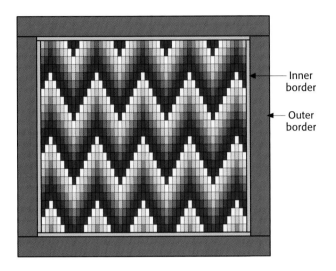

Inner border

Outer border

When you need to make a long inner border strip, join the strips with a diagonal seam in order to conserve fabric.

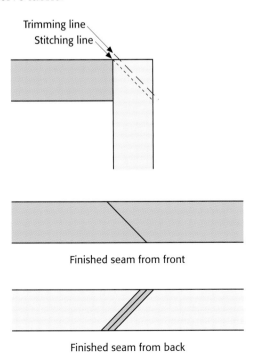

Trimming line
Stitching line

Finished seam from front

Finished seam from back

Add the top and bottom borders last. This allows you the option of an "Easy (No Hand-Sewing) Sleeve," as described on page 89. The following steps describe the process of adding borders.

1. Measure the center of your quilt top from top to bottom to determine its finished length.
2. Cut the strips for the side borders to match the measurements of your quilt. Join inner border strips with a diagonal seam, if necessary, to arrive at the length you need.

## TIP:
When pinning border strips to your quilt top, pin the middle of the strip first and then at either end. The next pins should go in between the end and the middle points. Continue dividing the space between pins until the border is secure for easy stitching. Pinning the border in this manner prevents the border strip from scooting down the quilt top as you sew and evenly distributes any excess fullness.

3. Sew the side borders to the quilt top. Next, measure the new width of the quilt top with the side borders added. Cut the top and bottom border strips to this measurement and sew them to the top and bottom of the quilt top.
4. If you have more than one border, sew the first border fabric on all 4 sides of the quilt before adding the next border fabric.
5. Press the seam allowances toward the borders, away from the center of the quilt. Always press each seam before adding the next border strip.
6. Repeat steps 1 through 5 for each additional border.

# GALLERY

POSITIVE IMPACT by Beth Ann Williams, 1998, Grand Rapids, Michigan, 53" x 64½".
From the collection of Barbara Williams Hulet.

In recognition of the impact one person can have on the world around her, this quilt honors Barbara Williams Hulet for her compassion, creativity, and dedication to the Atlanta, Georgia, community affected by the AIDS virus. It also commemorates a dear friend of mine who passed away from AIDS.

STARRY, STARRY NIGHT by Beth Ann Williams, 1998, Grand Rapids, Michigan, 69½" x 41".
From the collection of Amy Logsdon.

This design closely resembles the traditional bargello needlepoint pattern "Aurora Borealis," although the peach-colored accent line flickering across the face of the quilt breaks with the formality of the original pattern. When I quilted this piece, I wanted to soften the rigid geometry of the needlepoint pattern. I thought about one of my favorite painters, Vincent Van Gogh (not known, I might say, for his subtlety). I especially love the swirling expressiveness of his *Starry Night*. This painting became the starting point for the free-motion quilting with endlessly swirling spirals in variegated rayon thread.

BOBBIE'S GARDEN by Bobbie J. Pillow, 2000, Romulus, Michigan, 79" x 83½".
From the collection of Frances Janow.

Bobbie used the pattern for "Monet's Garden" (see page 56) to make this wonderful bed-sized version for her mother, Frances Janow. To increase the width of the quilt, she attached three additional vertical rows of bargello segments to the design. To increase the length of the quilt, she made two identical versions of the bargello pattern (including the extra rows) and sewed them together. (Unless it is a medallion design, such as "Enchanted Carpet" on page 80, any bargello pattern in this book can be adjusted in the same manner. The bottom of one bargello section will always match up perfectly with the top of an identical bargello section.)

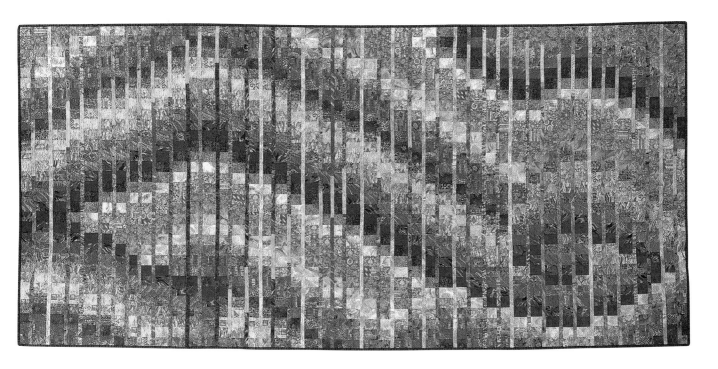

DREAMING OF THE ANCIENT ONES by Beth Ann Williams, 1997, Grand Rapids, Michigan, 100" x 46½".

The main design line of this piece (the darkest purple fabric) was inspired by the eye and brow of an elusive face appearing (and seeming to disappear) on certain Celtic artifacts in the La Tène–style, dating from approximately 300 B.C. to 100 A.D. The dramatic play of light and color is my response to the powerful, colorful, and passionate nature of the ancient Celtic peoples—tangible yet elusive.

ISLAND OF THE BLUE TURTLES by Beth Ann Williams, 1998, Grand Rapids, Michigan, 63" x 70".

The inspiration for this quilt was the music of Sting, and Marge Edie's quilt "Moonlight and Roses," published in her book *Bargello Quilts* (That Patchwork Place, 1994). As I expanded the design and worked in an entirely new palette of colors and textures, some very interesting things began to happen. A strong musical quality is evident in this piece—sometimes moody, sometimes sparkling and joyful. And as the colors and shapes interact with each other, different illusions are created—piercing light, crashing waves, the wingspan of a bird of mythic proportions.

# PROJECTS

# FIRE ON THE SAVANNAH

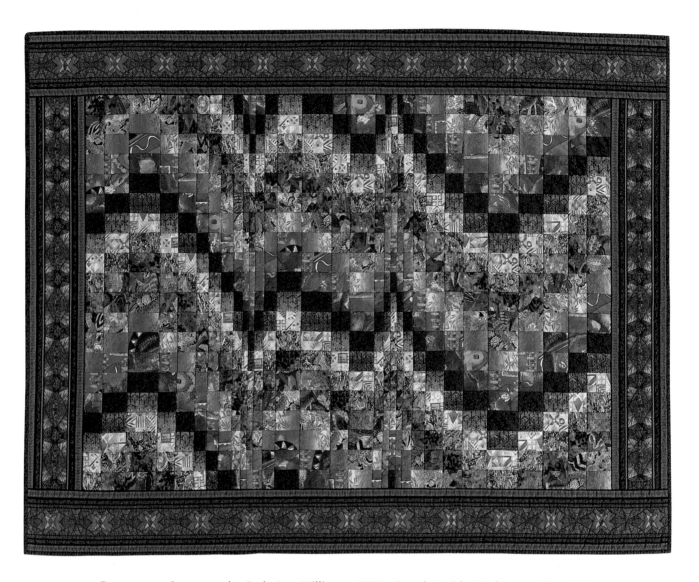

FIRE ON THE SAVANNAH by Beth Ann Williams, 1997, Grand Rapids, Michigan, 52" x 41".

The first in my Under African Skies series ("After the Rains" on page 48 is the second one), "Fire on the Savannah" was an attempt to deal with recurring nightmares I had about a specific event that occurred when I was growing up in Africa. Part of the growing cycle in the semiarid Sahel region where we lived is the regular burning of the fields in preparation for the next planting. On one particular day, the winds were up and the fires got out of control. The fires came so close to our home that some of the hair was actually singed off the faces of my father and the other men who were working desperately to divert the flames before they surrounded us completely. It is interesting to note that the nightmares stopped when this quilt was completed.

# MATERIALS   42"-wide fabric

⅜ yd. *each* of 10 fabrics for bargello repeating runs. Each strip set will include 2 strips from each fabric.

1⅝ yds. for border

1⅝ yds. for backing

½ yd. for binding

44" x 56" piece of batting

# CUTTING

Cut strips on the crosswise grain (from selvage to selvage) unless otherwise stated. All measurements include ¼"-wide seam allowances.

**From *each* of the 10 bargello fabrics, cut:**

4 strips, each 2" wide

**From the border fabric, cut:**

2 strips on the lengthwise grain, each 5¼" wide, for the side borders*

2 strips on the lengthwise grain, each 5¼" wide, for the top and bottom borders*

**From the binding fabric, cut:**

5 strips, each 2½" wide

*You will adjust the length of the border strips after you have completed the bargello section.

# MAKING THE QUILT

You will need 2 identical strip sets for this quilt. One strip set will have its seam allowances pressed toward the first strip, and the other will have its seam allowances pressed toward the last strip.

1. This quilt uses repeating runs in the strip sets. To create each strip set, lay out 10 strips for the first run. Then repeat the same 10 fabrics in the same order for the repeating run. Label and sew strip sets as described in "Sewing the Strip Sets" on page 32.

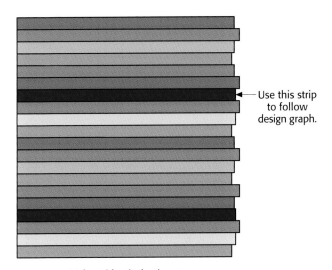

← Use this strip to follow design graph.

Make 2 identical strip sets.
Press seam allowances of first strip set toward top strip; press seam allowances of second strip set toward bottom strip.

2. With the first strip set, create a tube by sewing the unsewn edge of the first strip to the unsewn edge of the last strip. Sew with right sides together. Repeat for the second strip set. You should have 2 tubes.

3. Cut and label the bargello segments as described in "Cutting the Bargello Segments" on page 34. Use the widths listed in the following segment charts.

## ODD-NUMBERED BARGELLO SEGMENTS

Cut loops for odd-numbered segments from the first tube. The total width of loops cut from the first tube is 30¾". All measurements include ¼"-wide seam allowances.

| Bargello segment number | Cut width |
|---|---|
| 1 | 1½" |
| 3 | 3" |
| 5 | 2" |
| 7 | 1½" |
| 9 | 1¼" |
| 11 | 1" |
| 13 | 1½" |
| 15 | 3" |
| 17 | 2½" |
| 19 | 1" |
| 21 | 1" |
| 23 | 1½" |
| 25 | 2" |
| 27 | 3" |
| 29 | 2½" |
| 31 | 2½" |

## EVEN-NUMBERED BARGELLO SEGMENTS

Cut loops for even-numbered segments from the second tube. The total width of loops cut from the second tube is 26¾". All measurements include ¼"-wide seam allowances.

| Bargello segment number | Cut width |
|---|---|
| 2 | 2½" |
| 4 | 2" |
| 6 | 1½" |
| 8 | 1½" |
| 10 | 1" |
| 12 | 1¼" |
| 14 | 2½" |
| 16 | 2" |
| 18 | 1¼" |
| 20 | 1" |
| 22 | 1¼" |
| 24 | 2" |
| 26 | 2½" |
| 28 | 2½" |
| 30 | 2" |

4. Open the bargello loops as described in "Laying Out the Body of the Quilt" on page 35. Shift the dominant fabric up or down one segment each time, following the movement of the design graph on page 47.

5. Move the masking-tape labels to the top of each bargello segment. Referring to "Laying Out the Body of the Quilt," lay out the segments to check the flow of the design. Confirm that all seam allowances have been pressed in the correct direction so they will butt against each other when the segments are sewn together.

6. Sew the bargello segments together as described in "Assembling the Body of the Quilt" on page 36.

7. As described in "Adding Borders" on page 36, sew the side, top, and bottom border strips to the bargello section.

8. Layer and baste the quilt top, batting, and backing. Quilt as desired. See "Choosing a Quilting Method" on page 85 for tried-and-true suggestions for quilting bargello quilts.

9. Square up the quilt sandwich as described in "Squaring Up" on page 88.

10. If desired, sew a display sleeve to the back of your quilt. See "Adding a Sleeve" on page 89.

11. Sew on the binding. See "Binding" on page 91 for detailed instructions.

12. Sign and date your work, and enjoy your creation!

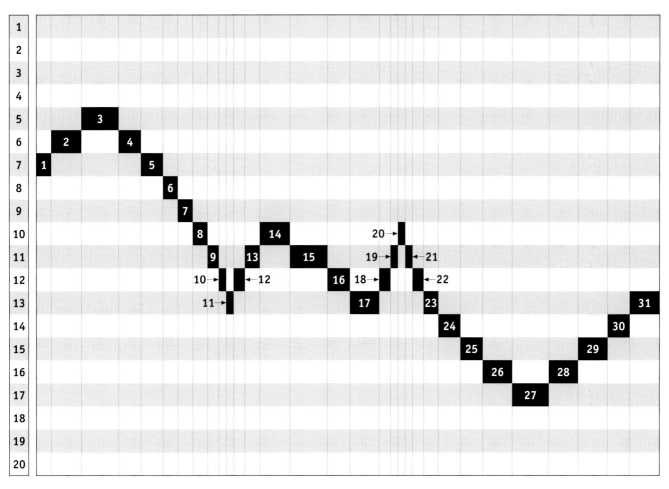

**Design graph**

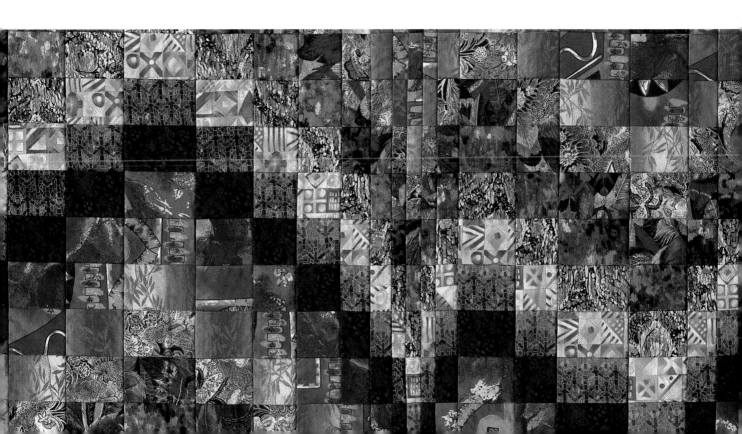

# AFTER THE RAINS

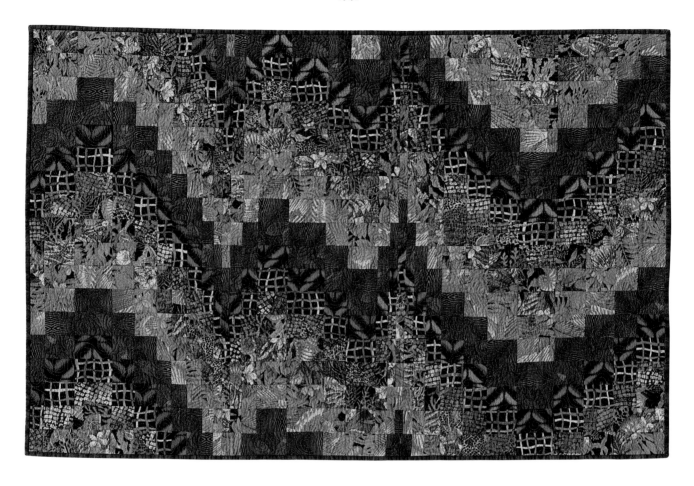

AFTER THE RAINS by Beth Ann Williams, 1997, Grand Rapids, Michigan, 41¼" x 26⅞".
From the collection of Diane M. Peffer.

This quilt is the second in my Under African Skies series and the antidote to "Fire on the Savannah." While living in Africa, I was always amazed at the transformation the landscape would undergo during the all-too-brief rainy season. The contrast between the wide-open, dusty plains of Chad and the dense equatorial jungle over the border into the Central African Republic was also an experience that filled me with wonder. It often seemed as if vibrant flashes of light and color were winking at me mysteriously as I passed by the jungle.

# MATERIALS   42"-wide fabric

⅜ yd. *each* of 9 fabrics for bargello repeating runs. Each strip set will include 2 strips from each fabric.

1½ yds. for backing

⅜ yd. for binding

31½" x 46½" piece of batting

# CUTTING

Cut strips on the crosswise grain (from selvage to selvage). All measurements include ¼"-wide seam allowances.

**From *each* of the 9 bargello fabrics, cut:**

4 strips, each 2" wide

**From the binding fabric, cut:**

4 strips, each 2½" wide

# MAKING THE QUILT

You will need 2 identical strip sets for this quilt. One strip set will have its seam allowances pressed toward the first strip, and the other will have its seam allowances pressed toward the last strip.

1. This quilt uses repeating runs in the strip sets. To create each strip set, lay out 9 strips for the first run. Then repeat the same 9 fabrics in the same order for the repeating run. Label and sew strip sets as described in "Sewing the Strip Sets" on page 32.

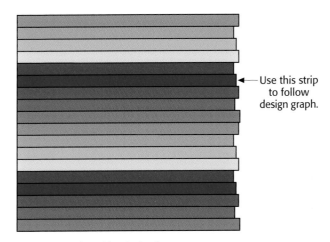

Use this strip to follow design graph.

Make 2 identical strip sets.
Press seam allowances of first strip set toward top strip; press seam allowances of second strip set toward bottom strip.

2. With the first strip set, create a tube by sewing the unsewn edge of the first strip to the unsewn edge of the last strip. Sew with right sides together. Repeat for the second strip set. You should have 2 tubes.

3. Cut and label the bargello segments as described in "Cutting the Bargello Segments" on page 34. Use the widths listed in the following segment charts.

## ODD-NUMBERED BARGELLO SEGMENTS

Cut loops for odd-numbered segments from the first tube. The total width of loops cut from the first tube is 30¾". All measurements include ¼"-wide seam allowances.

| Bargello segment number | Cut width |
|---|---|
| 1 | 1½" |
| 3 | 3" |
| 5 | 2" |
| 7 | 1½" |
| 9 | 1¼" |
| 11 | 1" |
| 13 | 1½" |
| 15 | 3" |
| 17 | 2½" |
| 19 | 1" |
| 21 | 1" |
| 23 | 1½" |
| 25 | 2" |
| 27 | 3" |
| 29 | 2½" |
| 31 | 2½" |

## EVEN-NUMBERED BARGELLO SEGMENTS

Cut loops for even-numbered segments from the second tube. The total width of loops cut from the second tube is 26¾". All measurements include ¼"-wide seam allowances.

| Bargello segment number | Cut width |
|---|---|
| 2 | 2½" |
| 4 | 2" |
| 6 | 1½" |
| 8 | 1½" |
| 10 | 1" |
| 12 | 1¼" |
| 14 | 2½" |
| 16 | 2" |
| 18 | 1¼ |
| 20 | 1" |
| 22 | 1¼" |
| 24 | 2" |
| 26 | 2½" |
| 28 | 2½" |
| 30 | 2" |

4. Open the bargello loops as described in "Laying Out the Body of the Quilt" on page 35. Shift the dominant fabric up or down one segment each time, following the movement of the design graph on page 51.

5. Move the masking-tape labels to the top of each bargello segment. Referring to "Laying Out the Body of the Quilt," lay out the segments to check the flow of the design. Confirm that all seam allowances have been pressed in the correct direction so they will butt against each other when the segments are sewn together.

6. Sew the bargello segments together as described in "Assembling the Body of the Quilt" on page 36.

7. Carefully press the completed bargello section.

8. Layer and baste the quilt top, batting, and backing. Quilt as desired. See "Choosing a Quilting Method" on page 85 for tried-and-true suggestions for quilting bargello quilts.

9. Square up the quilt sandwich as described in "Squaring Up" on page 88.

10. If desired, sew a display sleeve to the back of your quilt. See "Adding a Sleeve" on page 89.

11. Sew on the binding. See "Binding" on page 91 for detailed instructions.

12. Sign and date your work, and enjoy your creation!

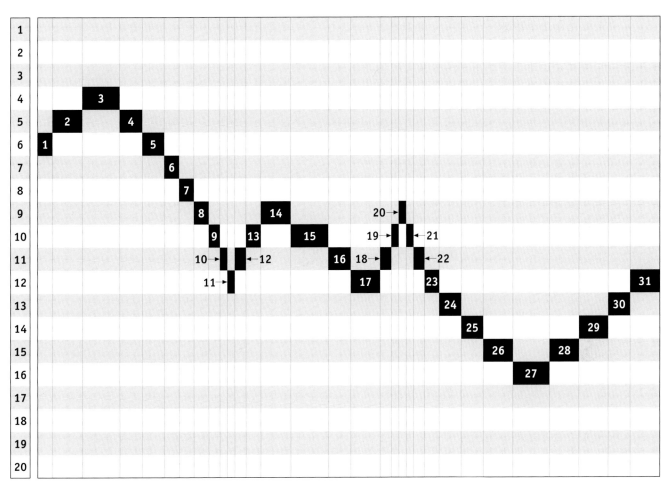

**Design graph**

# CASCADE

CASCADE by Pam Crans and Beth Ann Williams, 2000, Grand Rapids, Michigan, 29" x 34½".

Tranquil blues ripple around and through this little quilt, punctuated by strong florals and deep burgundies. It doesn't take long to make "Cascade," which means that it is a wonderful pattern for beginners. It is a great way to get your feet wet, playing with colors and textures.

# MATERIALS 42"-wide fabric

¼ yd. *each* of 19 fabrics for bargello segments (fat quarters work well for this project)
1 yd. for border
1 yd. for backing
⅜ yd. for binding
34½" x 41" piece of batting

# CUTTING

Cut strips on the crosswise grain (from selvage to selvage) unless otherwise stated. All measurements include ¼"-wide seam allowances.

**From *each* of the 19 bargello-segment fabrics, cut:**
2 strips, each 2" x 21"

**From the border fabric, cut:**
2 strips on the lengthwise grain, each 4¼" wide, for side borders*
2 strips on the lengthwise grain, each 4¼" wide, for top and bottom borders*

**From the binding fabric, cut:**
4 strips, each 2½" wide

*You will adjust the length of the border strips after you have completed the bargello section.

# MAKING THE QUILT

You will need 2 identical strip sets for this quilt. One strip set will have its seam allowances pressed toward the first strip, and the other will have its seam allowances pressed toward the last strip.

1. Label and sew strip sets as described in "Sewing the Strip Sets" on page 32.

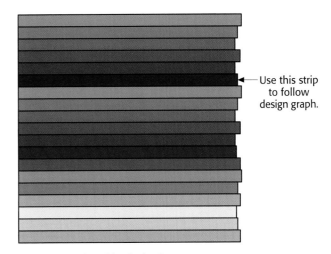

← Use this strip to follow design graph.

Make 2 identical strip sets.
Press seam allowances of first strip set toward top strip; press seam allowances of second strip set toward bottom strip.

2. With the first strip set, create a tube by sewing the unsewn edge of the first strip to the unsewn edge of the last strip. Sew with right sides together. Repeat for the second strip set. You should have 2 tubes.
3. Cut and label the bargello segments as described in "Cutting the Bargello Segments" on page 34. Use the widths listed in the following segment charts.

## ODD-NUMBERED BARGELLO SEGMENTS

Cut loops for odd-numbered segments from the first tube. The total width of loops cut from the first tube is 17¼". All measurements include ¼"-wide seam allowances.

| Bargello segment number | Cut width |
|---|---|
| 1 | 2¾" |
| 3 | 2" |
| 5 | 1¼" |
| 7 | 1¼" |
| 9 | 2" |
| 11 | 2" |
| 13 | 2¾" |
| 15 | 2" |
| 17 | 1¼" |

## EVEN-NUMBERED BARGELLO SEGMENTS

Cut loops for even-numbered segments from the second tube. The total width of loops cut from the second tube is 14¼". All measurements include ¼"-wide seam allowances.

| Bargello segment number | Cut width |
|---|---|
| 2 | 2" |
| 4 | 1¼" |
| 6 | 1¼" |
| 8 | 1¼" |
| 10 | 1¼" |
| 12 | 2¾" |
| 14 | 2" |
| 16 | 1¼" |
| 18 | 1¼" |

4. Open the bargello loops as described in "Laying Out the Body of the Quilt" on page 35. Shift the dominant fabric up or down one segment each time, following the movement of the design graph on page 55.

5. Move the masking-tape labels to the top of each bargello segment. Referring to "Laying Out the Body of the Quilt," lay out the segments to check the flow of the design. Confirm that all seam allowances have been pressed in the correct direction so they will butt against each other when the segments are sewn together.

6. Sew the bargello segments together as described in "Assembling the Body of the Quilt" on page 36.

7. As described in "Adding Borders" on page 36, sew the side, top, and bottom border strips to the bargello section.

8. Layer and baste the quilt top, batting, and backing. Quilt as desired. See "Choosing a Quilting Method" on page 85 for tried-and-true suggestions for quilting bargello quilts.

9. Square up the quilt sandwich as described in "Squaring Up" on page 88.

10. If desired, sew a display sleeve to the back of your quilt. See "Adding a Sleeve" on page 89.

11. Sew on the binding. See "Binding" on page 91 for detailed instructions.

12. Sign and date your work, and enjoy your creation!

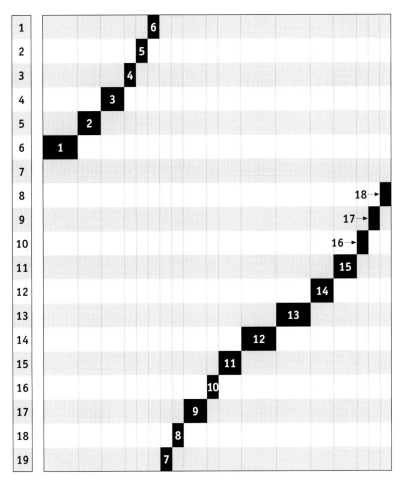

**Design graph**

# MONET'S GARDEN

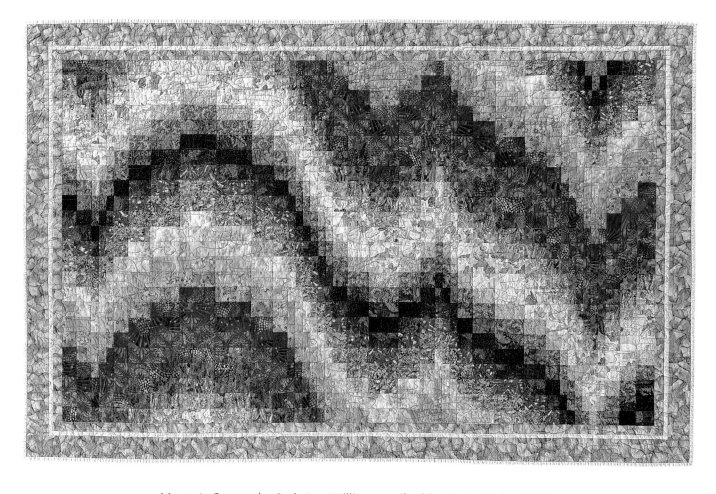

MONET'S GARDEN by Beth Ann Williams, quilted by Terrie Wicks, 2000,
Grand Rapids, Michigan, 67¼" x 43".

The origins of the palette for this quilt—Claude Monet's famous water lilies series—will be familiar to many. The quilting pattern further carries out the theme of rippling water. This design adapts well for a bed-sized quilt, like "Bobbie's Garden" on page 40.

# MATERIALS    42"-wide fabric

¼ yd. *each* of 24 fabrics for bargello segments
¼ yd. for inner border
¼ yd. for middle accent border
⅞ yd. for outer border
3 yds. for backing
½ yd. for binding
50½" x 75¾" piece of batting

# CUTTING

Cut strips on the crosswise grain (from selvage to selvage) unless otherwise stated. All measurements include ¼"-wide seam allowances.

**From *each* of the 24 bargello-segment fabrics, cut:**
2 strips, each 2" wide

**From the inner border fabric, cut:**
5 strips, each 1½" wide*

**From the middle accent border fabric, cut:**
6 strips, each 1" wide*

**From the outer border fabric, cut:**
2 strips on the lengthwise grain, each 4" wide, for outer side borders*
2 strips on the lengthwise grain, each 4" wide, for outer top and bottom borders*

**From the backing fabric, cut:**
2 pieces, each 51" x 42"

**From the binding fabric, cut:**
6 strips, each 2½" wide

*You will adjust the length of the border strips after you have completed the bargello section.

# MAKING THE QUILT

You will need 2 identical strip sets for this quilt. One strip set will have its seam allowances pressed toward the first strip, and the other will have its seam allowances pressed toward the last strip.

1. Label and sew strip sets as described in "Sewing the Strip Sets" on page 32.

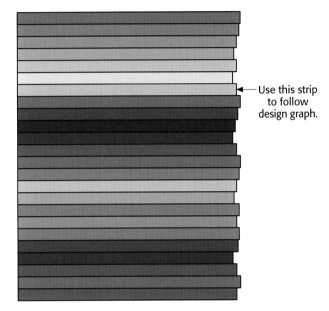

← Use this strip to follow design graph.

Make 2 identical strip sets.
Press seam allowances of first strip set toward top strip; press seam allowances of second strip set toward bottom strip.

2. With the first strip set, create a tube by sewing the unsewn edge of the first strip to the unsewn edge of the last strip. Sew with right sides together. Repeat for the second strip set. You should have 2 tubes.
3. Cut and label the bargello segments as described in "Cutting the Bargello Segments" on page 34. Use the widths listed in the following segment charts.

## ODD-NUMBERED BARGELLO SEGMENTS

Cut loops for odd-numbered segments from the first tube. The total width of loops cut from the first tube is 40". All measurements include ¼"-wide seam allowances.

| Bargello segment number | Cut width |
| --- | --- |
| 1 | 2" |
| 3 | 1¼" |
| 5 | 1¼" |
| 7 | 2¾" |
| 9 | 4¼" |
| 11 | 2¾" |
| 13 | 1¼" |
| 15 | 1¼" |
| 17 | 1¼" |
| 19 | 2" |
| 21 | 3½" |
| 23 | 2" |
| 25 | 1¼" |
| 27 | 2" |
| 29 | 3½" |
| 31 | 2" |
| 33 | 1¼" |
| 35 | 1¼" |
| 37 | 1¼" |
| 39 | 2" |

## EVEN-NUMBERED BARGELLO SEGMENTS

Cut loops for even-numbered segments from the second tube. The total width of loops cut from the second tube is 40". All measurements include ¼"-wide seam allowances.

| Bargello segment number | Cut width |
| --- | --- |
| 2 | 2" |
| 4 | 1¼" |
| 6 | 2" |
| 8 | 3½" |
| 10 | 3½" |
| 12 | 2" |
| 14 | 1¼" |
| 16 | 1¼" |
| 18 | 1¼" |
| 20 | 2¾" |
| 22 | 2¾" |
| 24 | 1¼" |
| 26 | 1¼" |
| 28 | 2¾" |
| 30 | 2¾" |
| 32 | 1¼" |
| 34 | 1¼" |
| 36 | 1¼" |
| 38 | 2" |
| 40 | 2¾" |

4. Open the bargello loops as described in "Laying Out the Body of the Quilt" on page 35. Shift the dominant fabric up or down one segment each time, following the movement of the design graph on page 59.

5. Move the masking-tape labels to the top of each bargello segment. Referring to "Laying Out the Body of the Quilt," lay out the segments to check the flow of the design. Confirm that all seam allowances have been pressed in the correct direction so they will butt against each other when the segments are sewn together.

6. Sew the bargello segments together as described in "Assembling the Body of the Quilt" on page 36.

7. As described in "Adding Borders" on page 36, sew the 5 inner border strips together on the diagonal to yield 1 long strip. Cut this strip as needed for the inner side, top, and bottom borders; sew the pieces to the bargello section. Repeat these steps with the 6 middle border strips. Sew the outer border strips to the quilt.

8. For the backing, sew the two 51" x 42" pieces together to make one 51" x 83½" piece. Trim the backing so it is 2" to 4" larger all around than your quilt top. Layer and baste the quilt top, batting, and backing. Quilt as desired. See "Choosing a Quilting Method" on page 85 for tried-and-true suggestions for quilting bargello quilts.

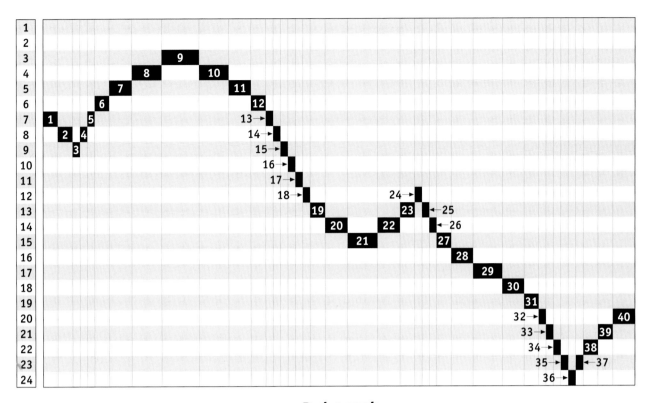

**Design graph**

9. Square up the quilt sandwich as described in "Squaring Up" on page 88.

10. If desired, sew a display sleeve to the back of your quilt. See "Adding a Sleeve" on page 89.

11. Sew on the binding. See "Binding" on page 91 for detailed instructions.

12. Sign and date your work, and enjoy your creation!

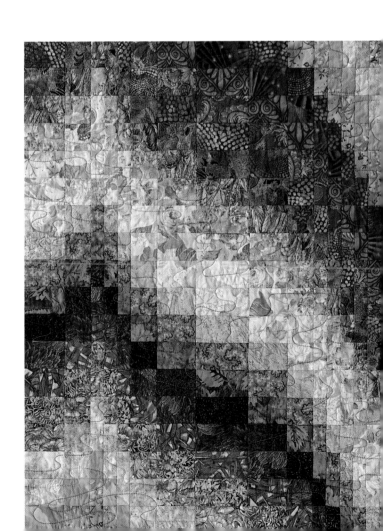

# AUTUMN GLOW

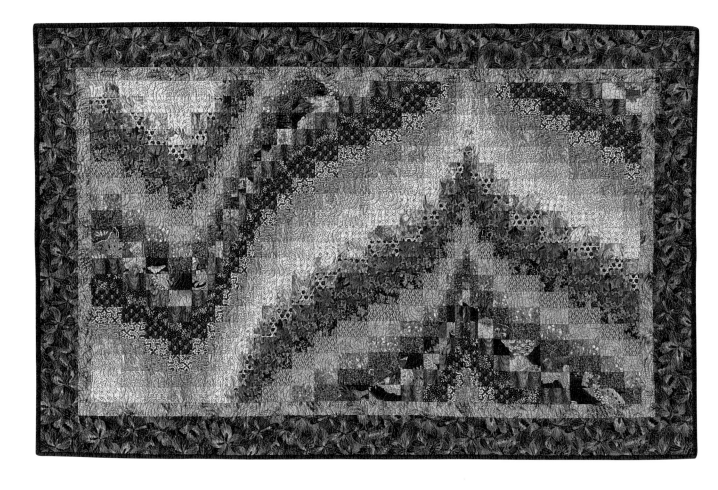

AUTUMN GLOW by Beth Ann Williams, 2000, Grand Rapids, Michigan, 60½" x 38½".

The sometimes-subtle, sometimes-bold richness of sunlit autumn leaves and tree-covered hillsides inspired the palette for this quilt.

# MATERIALS   42"-wide fabric

¼ yd. *each* of 20 fabrics for bargello segments
⅜ yd. for inner border
1⅞ yds. for outer border
2⅛ yds. for backing
⅝ yd. for binding
44" x 68" piece of batting

# CUTTING

Cut strips on the crosswise grain (from selvage to selvage) unless otherwise stated. All measurements include ¼"-wide seam allowances.

**From *each* of the 20 bargello-segment fabrics, cut:**
2 strips, each 2" wide

**From the inner border fabric, cut:**
5 strips, each 1¾" wide*

**From the outer border fabric, cut:**
2 strips on the lengthwise grain, each 4½" wide, for outer side borders*
2 strips on the lengthwise grain, each 4½" wide, for outer top and bottom borders*

**From the backing fabric, cut:**
1 piece, 42" x 66"

**From the binding fabric, cut:**
6 strips, each 2½" wide

*You will adjust the length of the border strips after you have completed the bargello section.

# MAKING THE QUILT

You will need 2 identical strip sets for this quilt. One strip set will have its seam allowances pressed toward the first strip, and the other will have its seam allowances pressed toward the last strip.

1. Label and sew strip sets as described in "Sewing the Strip Sets" on page 32.

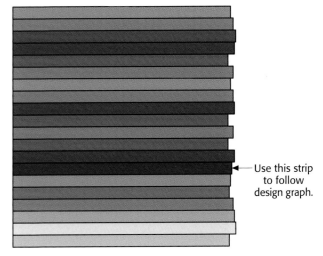

Use this strip to follow design graph.

Make 2 identical strip sets.
Press seam allowances of first strip set toward top strip; press seam allowances of second strip set toward bottom strip.

2. With the first strip set, create a tube by sewing the unsewn edge of the first strip to the unsewn edge of the last strip. Sew with right sides together. Repeat for the second strip set. You should have 2 tubes.
3. Cut and label the bargello segments as described in "Cutting the Bargello Segments" on page 34. Use the widths listed in the following segment charts.

## Odd-Numbered Bargello Segments

Cut loops for odd-numbered segments from the first tube. The total width of loops cut from the first tube is 35". All measurements include ¼"-wide seam allowances.

| Bargello segment number | Cut width |
|---|---|
| 1 | 3½" |
| 3 | 2¾" |
| 5 | 2" |
| 7 | 1¼" |
| 9 | 1¼" |
| 11 | 1¼" |
| 13 | 2" |
| 15 | 2¾" |
| 17 | 3½" |
| 19 | 2¾" |
| 21 | 1¼" |
| 23 | 1¼" |
| 25 | 1¼" |
| 27 | 2" |
| 29 | 3½" |
| 31 | 2¾" |

## Even-Numbered Bargello Segments

Cut loops for even-numbered segments from the second tube. The total width of loops cut from the second tube is 34¼". All measurements include ¼"-wide seam allowances.

| Bargello segment number | Cut width |
|---|---|
| 2 | 2¾" |
| 4 | 2¾" |
| 6 | 1¼" |
| 8 | 1¼" |
| 10 | 1¼" |
| 12 | 1¼" |
| 14 | 2" |
| 16 | 2¾" |
| 18 | 3½" |
| 20 | 2" |
| 22 | 1¼" |
| 24 | 1¼" |
| 26 | 2" |
| 28 | 3½" |
| 30 | 3½" |
| 32 | 2" |

4. Open the bargello loops as described in "Laying Out the Body of the Quilt" on page 35. Shift the dominant fabric up or down one segment each time, following the movement of the design graph on page 63.

5. Move the masking-tape labels to the top of each bargello segment. Referring to "Laying Out the Body of the Quilt," lay out the segments to check the flow of the design. Confirm that all seam allowances have been pressed in the correct direction so they will butt against each other when the segments are sewn together.

6. Sew the bargello segments together as described in "Assembling the Body of the Quilt" on page 36.

7. As described in "Adding Borders" on page 36, sew the 5 inner border strips together on the diagonal to yield 1 long strip. Cut this strip as needed for the inner side, top, and bottom borders; sew the pieces to the bargello section. Finally, sew the outer border strips to the quilt.

8. The 42" x 66" backing may not give a full 2" of excess fabric all around, but it should be sufficient. Layer and baste the quilt top, batting, and backing. Quilt as desired. See "Choosing a Quilting Method" on page 85 for tried-and-true suggestions for quilting bargello quilts.

9. Square up the quilt sandwich as described in "Squaring Up" on page 88.

10. If desired, sew a display sleeve to the back of your quilt. See "Adding a Sleeve" on page 89.

11. Sew on the binding. See "Binding" on page 91 for detailed instructions.

12. Sign and date your work, and enjoy your creation!

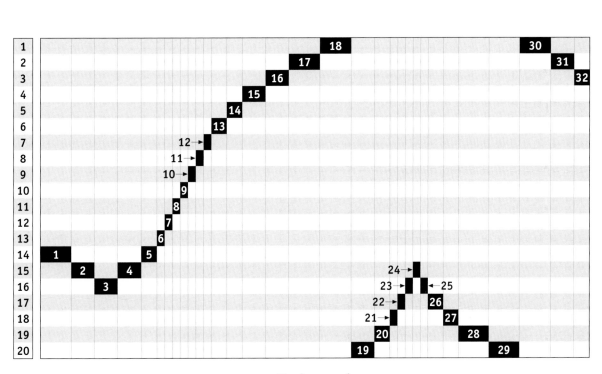

**Design graph**

# JOURNEY TO BYZANTIUM

JOURNEY TO BYZANTIUM by Beth Ann Williams, 1999, Grand Rapids, Michigan, 72" x 47½".

Like so many others, I am a passionately curious person, endlessly fascinated by the study of history, sociology, religion, and philosophy and how these are reflected in the art and craft of specific times, places, and peoples. For me, this quilt embodies an archetypal journey. Red and gold represent glittering wealth, fiery destruction, jewels, or embers.

# MATERIALS  42"-wide fabric

⅜ yd. *each* of 11 fabrics for bargello reverse-repeating runs. Select fabrics with values ranging from light to dark and back to light. (Each strip set will have reverse-repeating runs that contain 2 strips each of these 11 fabrics.)

¼ yd. *each* of 2 fabrics for highlights between the bargello reverse-repeating runs. Select fabrics with values lighter than any of the 11 reverse-repeating run fabrics.

½ yd. for inner border
½ yd. for middle border
2¼ yds. for outer border
3¼ yds. for backing
⅝ yd. for binding
54" x 80" piece of batting

# CUTTING

Cut strips on the crosswise grain (from selvage to selvage) unless otherwise stated. All measurements include ¼"-wide seam allowances.

**From *each* of the 11 bargello fabrics, cut:**
  4 strips, each 2" wide

**From *each* of the 2 highlight fabrics, cut:**
  2 strips, each 2" wide

**From the inner border fabric, cut:**
  2 strips, each 1¾" wide, for inner side borders*
  3 strips, each 1¾" wide, for inner top and bottom borders*

**From the middle border fabric, cut:**
  2 strips, each 2¼" wide, for middle side borders*
  4 strips, each 2¼" wide, for middle top and bottom borders*

**From the outer border fabric, cut:**
  2 strips on the lengthwise grain, each 4¼" wide, for outer side borders*
  2 strips on the lengthwise grain, each 4¼" wide, for outer top and bottom borders*

**From the backing fabric, cut:**
  2 pieces, each 56" x 42"

**From the binding fabric, cut:**
  7 strips, each 2½" wide

*You will adjust the length of the border strips after you have completed the bargello section.

# MAKING THE QUILT

You will need 2 identical strip sets for this quilt. One strip set will have its seam allowances pressed toward the first strip, and the other will have its seam allowances pressed toward the last strip.

1. This quilt uses reverse-repeating runs in the strip sets. To create the first strip set, lay out the first 11 strips and 1 highlight strip. Repeat the 11 fabrics in reverse order and add a second highlight strip. Lay out your second strip set the same way. Label and sew strip sets as described in "Sewing the Strip Sets" on page 32.

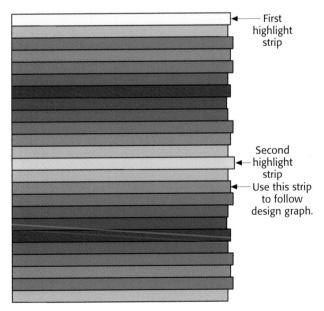

First highlight strip

Second highlight strip

Use this strip to follow design graph.

Make 2 identical strip sets.
Press seam allowances of first strip set toward top strip; press seam allowances of second strip set toward bottom strip.

## Odd-Numbered Bargello Segments

Cut loops for odd-numbered segments from the first tube. The total width of loops cut from the first tube is 40½". All measurements include ¼"-wide seam allowances.

| Bargello segment number | Cut width |
|---|---|
| 1 | 2¾" |
| 3 | 2" |
| 5 | 1¼" |
| 7 | 2" |
| 9 | 2¾" |
| 11 | 4¼" |
| 13 | 2¾" |
| 15 | 1¼" |
| 17 | 1¼" |
| 19 | 2" |
| 21 | 3½" |
| 23 | 2" |
| 25 | 1¼" |
| 27 | 1¼" |
| 29 | 2" |
| 31 | 3½" |
| 33 | 2¾" |
| 35 | 2" |

## Even-Numbered Bargello Segments

Cut loops for even-numbered segments from the second tube. The total width of loops cut from the second tube is 38¼". All measurements include ¼"-wide seam allowances.

| Bargello segment number | Cut width |
|---|---|
| 2 | 2¾" |
| 4 | 2" |
| 6 | 1¼" |
| 8 | 2" |
| 10 | 3½" |
| 12 | 3½" |
| 14 | 2" |
| 16 | 1¼" |
| 18 | 1¼" |
| 20 | 2¾" |
| 22 | 2¾" |
| 24 | 2" |
| 26 | 1¼" |
| 28 | 1¼ |
| 30 | 2¾" |
| 32 | 3½" |
| 34 | 2½" |

2. With the first strip set, create a tube by sewing the unsewn edge of the first strip to the unsewn edge of the last strip. Sew with right sides together. Repeat for the second strip set. You should have 2 tubes.

3. Cut and label the bargello segments as described in "Cutting the Bargello Segments" on page 34. Use the widths listed in the segment charts above.

4. Open the bargello loops as described in "Laying Out the Body of the Quilt" on page 35. Shift the dominant fabric up or down one segment each time, following the movement of the design graph on page 67.

5. Move the masking-tape labels to the top of each bargello segment. Referring to "Laying Out the Body of the Quilt," lay out the segments to check the flow of the design. Confirm that all seam allowances have been pressed in the correct direction so they will butt against each other when the sgements are sewn together.

6. Sew the bargello segments together as described in "Assembling the Body of the Quilt" on page 36.

7. As described in "Adding Borders" on page 36, sew 2 inner border strips to the sides of the bargello section. Then sew the remaining 3 inner border strips together on the diagonal to yield 1 long strip. Cut this long strip into 2 strips for the inner top and bottom borders; sew these pieces to the bargello section.

For the middle border, sew 1 middle border strip to each side of the quilt top. Sew the remaining 4 middle border strips into pairs to yield 2 long strips. Sew these long strips to the top and bottom of the quilt top. Finally, sew the outer border strips to the quilt.

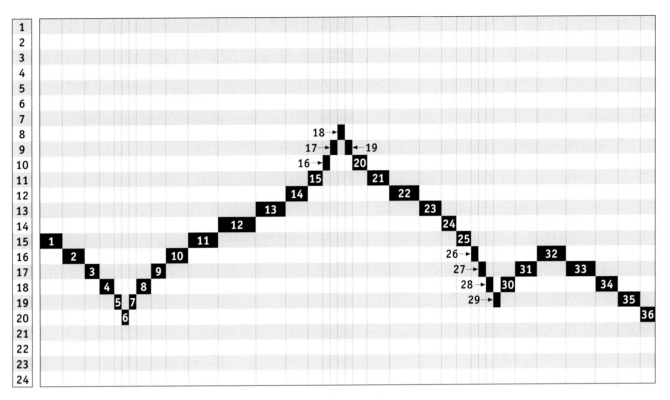

**Design graph**

8. For the backing, sew the two 56" x 42" pieces together to make one 56" x 83½" piece. Trim the backing so it is 2" to 4" larger all around than your quilt top. Layer and baste the quilt top, batting, and backing. Quilt as desired. See "Choosing a Quilting Method" on page 85 for tried-and-true suggestions for quilting bargello quilts.

9. Square up the quilt sandwich as described in "Squaring Up" on page 88.

10. If desired, sew a display sleeve to the back of your quilt. See "Adding a Sleeve" on page 89.

11. Sew on the binding. See "Binding" on page 91 for detailed instructions.

12. Sign and date your work, and enjoy your creation!

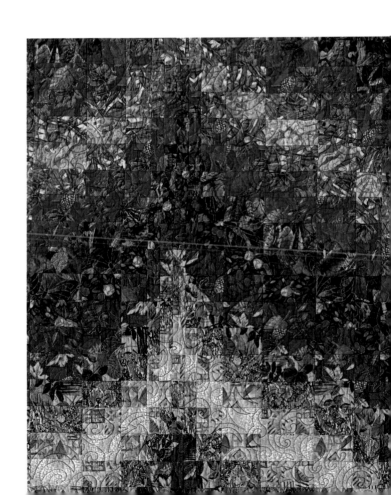

# AURORA

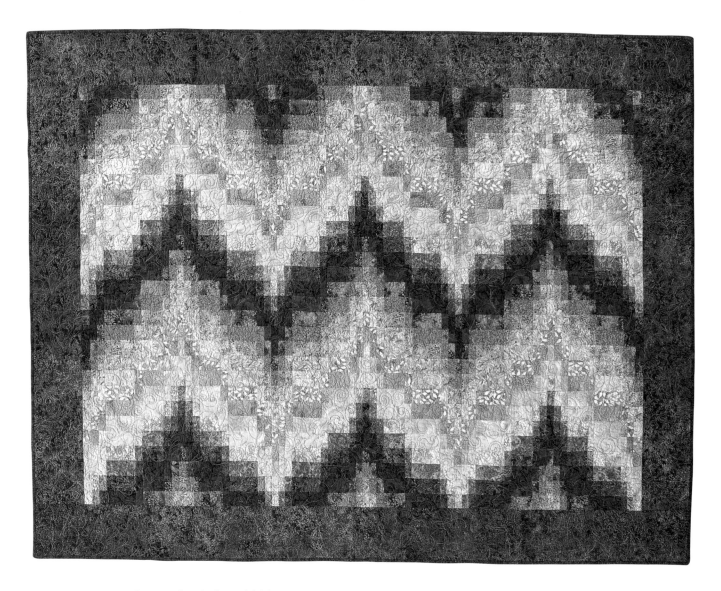

AURORA by Cathy Babbidge and Beth Ann Williams, quilted by Terrie Wicks, 2000,
Grand Rapids, Michigan, 86½" x 67¼".

This quilt is another variation on the traditional needlepoint bargello pattern "Aurora Borealis." (See "Starry, Starry Night" on page 39 for a more complex version.) I intend to use this quilt as a stunning wall hanging; however, it also fits nicely lengthwise on a twin-sized bed. To make a full or queen-sized coverlet, make two bargello sections exactly as indicated in the pattern, and then sew the bottom of the first section to the top of the second bargello section. (The design lines will match up exactly.) See "Bobbie's Garden" on page 40 for an example of another quilt enlarged in this manner.

# MATERIALS 42"-wide fabric

⅝ yd. *each* of 14 fabrics for the bargello repeating runs. Each strip set will include 2 strips from each fabric.
2¾ yds. for border
5¾ yds. for backing
¾ yd. for binding
74" x 97" piece of batting

# CUTTING

Cut strips on the crosswise grain (from selvage to selvage) unless otherwise stated. All measurements include ¼"-wide seam allowances.

**From *each* of the 14 bargello fabrics, cut:**
6 strips, each 2½" wide

**From the border fabric, cut:**
2 strips on the lengthwise grain, each 7¼" wide, for side borders*
2 strips on the lengthwise grain, each 7¼" wide, for top and bottom borders*

**From the backing fabric, cut:**
2 pieces, each 42" x 99"

**From the binding fabric, cut:**
9 strips, each 2¼" wide

*You will adjust the length of the border strips after you have completed the bargello section.

# MAKING THE QUILT

You will need 3 identical strip sets for this quilt. One strip set will have its seam allowances pressed toward the first strip, and the other 2 will have their seam allowances pressed toward the last strip.

1. This quilt uses repeating runs in the strip sets. To create each strip set, lay out 14 strips for the first run. Then repeat the same 14 fabrics in the same order for the repeating run. Label and sew strip sets as described in "Sewing the Strip Sets" on page 32.

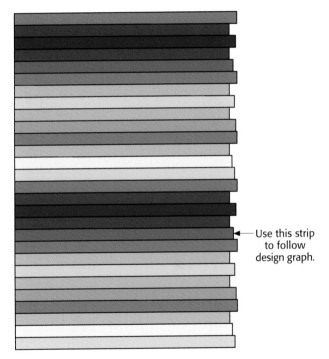

← Use this strip to follow design graph.

Make 3 identical strip sets.
Press seam allowances of first strip set toward top strip; press seam allowances of second and third strip sets toward bottom strip.

2. With the first strip set, create a tube by sewing the unsewn edge of the first strip to the unsewn edge of the last strip. Sew with right sides together. Repeat for the second and third strip sets. You should have 3 tubes.
3. Cut and label the bargello segments as described in "Cutting the Bargello Segments" on page 34. Use the widths listed in the following segment charts.

## ODD-NUMBERED BARGELLO SEGMENTS

Cut loops for odd-numbered segments from the first tube. The total width of loops cut from the first tube is 38". All measurements include ¼"-wide seam allowances.

| Bargello segment number | Cut width |
|:---:|:---:|
| 1 | 1¾" |
| 3 | 1½" |
| 5 | 1½" |
| 7 | 1½" |
| 9 | 1½" |
| 11 | 1½" |
| 13 | 1½" |
| 15 | 1½" |
| 17 | 1½" |
| 19 | 1½" |
| 21 | 1½" |
| 23 | 1½" |
| 25 | 1½" |
| 27 | 1½" |
| 29 | 1½" |
| 31 | 1½" |
| 33 | 1½" |
| 35 | 1½" |
| 37 | 1½" |
| 39 | 1½" |
| 41 | 1½" |
| 43 | 1½" |
| 45 | 1½" |
| 47 | 1½" |
| 49 | 1¾" |

## EVEN-NUMBERED BARGELLO SEGMENTS

Cut loops for even-numbered segments from the second and third tubes. The total width of loops cut from the second and third tubes is 66". All measurements include ¼"-wide seam allowances.

| Bargello segment number | Cut width |
|:---:|:---:|
| 2 | 1½" |
| 4 | 4½" |
| 6 | 3½" |
| 8 | 1½" |
| 10 | 1½" |
| 12 | 3½" |
| 14 | 4½" |
| 16 | 1½" |
| 18 | 1½" |
| 20 | 4½" |
| 22 | 3½" |
| 24 | 1½" |
| 26 | 1½" |
| 28 | 3½" |
| 30 | 4½" |
| 32 | 1½" |
| 34 | 1½" |
| 36 | 4½" |
| 38 | 3½" |
| 40 | 1½" |
| 42 | 1½" |
| 44 | 3½" |
| 46 | 4½" |
| 48 | 1½" |

4. Open the bargello loops as described in "Laying Out the Body of the Quilt" on page 35. Shift the dominant fabric up or down one segment each time, following the movement of the design graph on page 71.

5. Move the masking-tape labels to the top of each bargello segment. Referring to "Laying Out the Body of the Quilt," lay out the segments to check the flow of the design. Confirm that all seam allowances have been pressed in the correct direction so they will butt against each other when the segments are sewn together.

6. Sew the bargello segments together as described in "Assembling the Body of the Quilt" on page 36.

7. As described in "Adding Borders" on page 36, sew the side, top, and bottom border strips to the bargello section.

8. For the backing, sew the two 42" x 99" pieces together to yield one piece 83½" x 99". Trim the backing so it is 2" to 4" larger all around than your quilt top. Layer and baste the quilt top, batting, and backing. Quilt as desired. See "Choosing a Quilting Method" on page 85 for

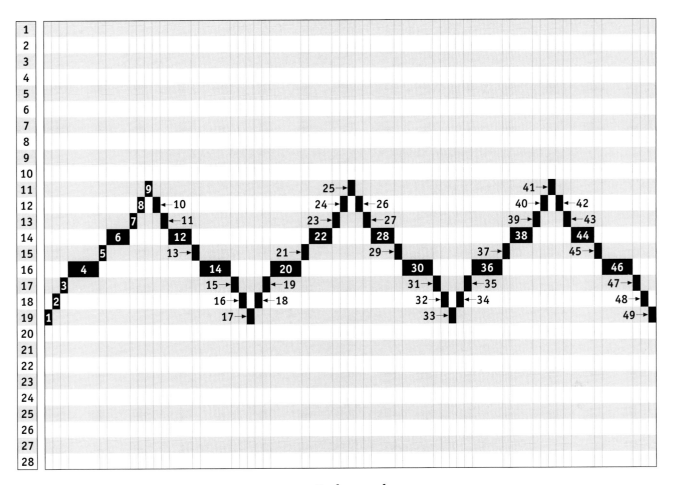

**Design graph**

tried-and-true suggestions for quilting bargello quilts.

9. Square up the quilt sandwich as described in "Squaring Up" on page 88.

10. If desired, sew a display sleeve to the back of your quilt. See "Adding a Sleeve" on page 89.

11. Sew on the binding. See "Binding" on page 91 for detailed instructions.

12. Sign and date your work, and enjoy your creation!

# STAR KINDLER

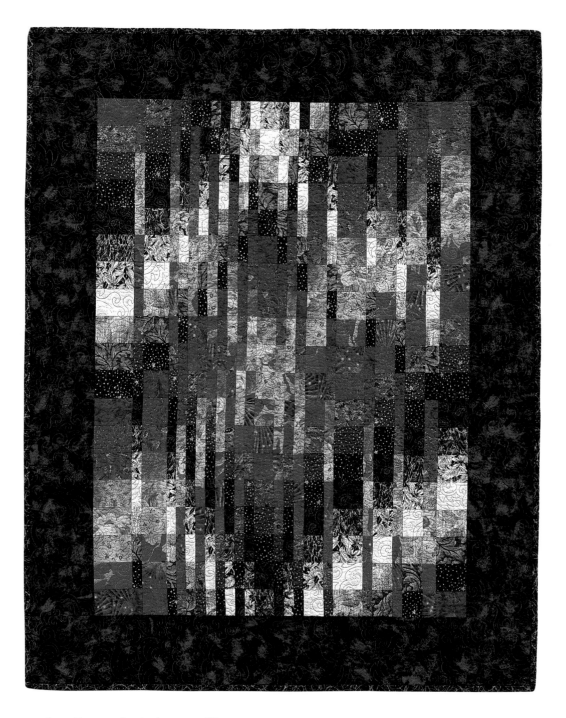

STAR KINDLER by Beth Ann Williams, 2000, Grand Rapids, Michigan, 38⅛" x 47⅞".

This piece took form after listening to "Star Kindler: A Celtic Conversation Across Time," by writer and recording artist Michael Card. Star Kindler is also an ancient name for the Creator of the Universe. There are two design lines here, converging in the middle of the quilt for maximum impact.

# MATERIALS   42"-wide fabric

¼ yd. *each* of 19 fabrics for bargello segments
1¼ yds. for border
1⅝ yds. for backing
½ yd. for binding
39½" x 53" piece of batting

# CUTTING

Cut strips on the crosswise grain (from selvage to selvage) unless otherwise stated. All measurements include ¼"-wide seam allowances.

**From *each* of the 19 bargello-segment fabrics, cut:**
2 strips, each 2½" x 42". Take 1 strip of each fabric and cut it in half to yield 2 strips, each 2½" x 22". You will have one 2½" x 22" strip left over from each fabric after you sew your strip sets.

**From the border fabric, cut:**
2 strips on the lengthwise grain, each 5¾" wide, for side borders*
2 strips on the lengthwise grain, each 5¾" wide, for top and bottom borders*

**From the backing fabric, cut:**
1 piece, 39½" x 53"

**From the binding fabric, cut:**
5 strips, each 2½" wide

*You will adjust the length of the border strips after you have completed the bargello section.

# MAKING THE QUILT

You will need 2 different-length strip sets for this quilt. One strip set will be made from the 42" strips with its seam allowances pressed toward the first strip. The other strip set will be made from the 22" strips with its seam allowances pressed toward the last strip.

1. Label and sew strip sets as described in "Sewing the Strip Sets" on page 32.

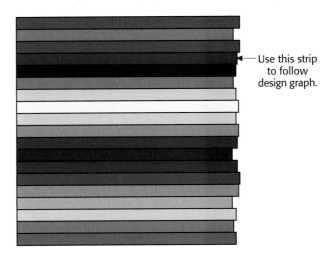

Use this strip to follow design graph.

Make 2 strip sets.
Press seam allowances of first strip set toward top strip; press seam allowances of second strip set toward bottom strip.

2. With the first strip set, create a tube by sewing the unsewn edge of the first strip to the unsewn edge of the last strip. Sew with right sides together. Repeat for the second strip set. You should have 2 tubes.
3. Cut and label the bargello segments as described in "Cutting the Bargello Segments" on page 34. Use the widths listed in the following segment charts.

## ODD-NUMBERED BARGELLO SEGMENTS

Cut loops for odd-numbered segments from the 42"-wide tube. The total width of loops cut from the first tube is 25¾". All measurements include ¼"-wide seam allowances.

| Bargello segment number | Cut width |
|---|---|
| 1 | 3½" |
| 3 | 2½" |
| 5 | 1¼" |
| 7 | 1¼" |
| 9 | 1¼" |
| 11 | 1¼" |
| 13 | 2" |
| 15 | 1¼" |
| 17 | 2" |
| 19 | 2¾" |
| 21 | 2" |
| 23 | 2" |
| 25 | 2¾" |

## EVEN-NUMBERED BARGELLO SEGMENTS

Cut loops for even-numbered segments from the 21" tube. The total width of loops cut from the second tube is 15¼". All measurements include ¼"-wide seam allowances.

| Bargello segment number | Cut width |
|---|---|
| 2 | 1¼" |
| 4 | 1¼" |
| 6 | 1¼" |
| 8 | 1¼" |
| 10 | 1¼" |
| 12 | 1¼" |
| 14 | 1¼" |
| 16 | 1¼" |
| 18 | 1¼" |
| 20 | 1¼" |
| 22 | 1¼" |
| 24 | 1½" |

4. Open the bargello loops as described in "Laying Out the Body of the Quilt" on page 35. Shift the dominant fabric up or down one segment each time, following the movement of the design graph on page 75.

5. Move the masking-tape labels to the top of each bargello segment. Referring to "Laying Out the Body of the Quilt," lay out the segments to check the flow of the design. Confirm that all seam allowances have been pressed in the correct direction so they will butt against each other when the segments are sewn together.

6. Sew the bargello segments together as described in "Assembling the Body of the Quilt" on page 36.

7. As described in "Adding Borders" on page 36, sew the side, top, and bottom border strips to the bargello section.

8. Layer and baste the quilt top, batting, and backing. Quilt as desired. See "Choosing a Quilting Method" on page 85 for tried-and-true suggestions for quilting bargello quilts.

9. Square up the quilt sandwich as described in "Squaring Up" on page 88.

10. If desired, sew a display sleeve to the back of your quilt. See "Adding a Sleeve" on page 89.

11. Sew on the binding. See "Binding" on page 91 for detailed instructions.

12. Sign and date your work, and enjoy your creation!

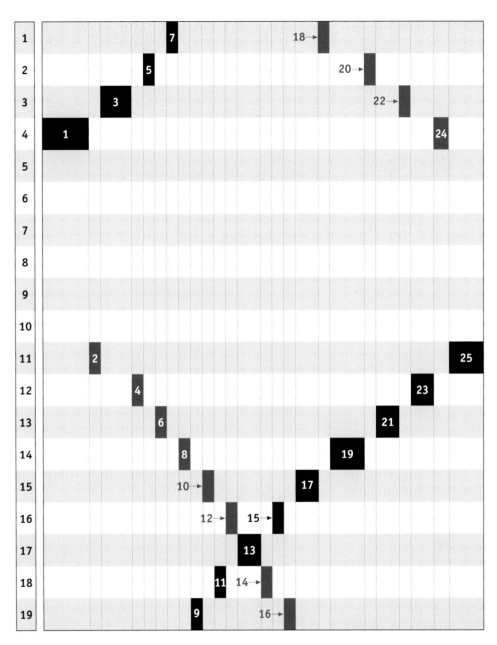

**Design graph**

# MIRAGE

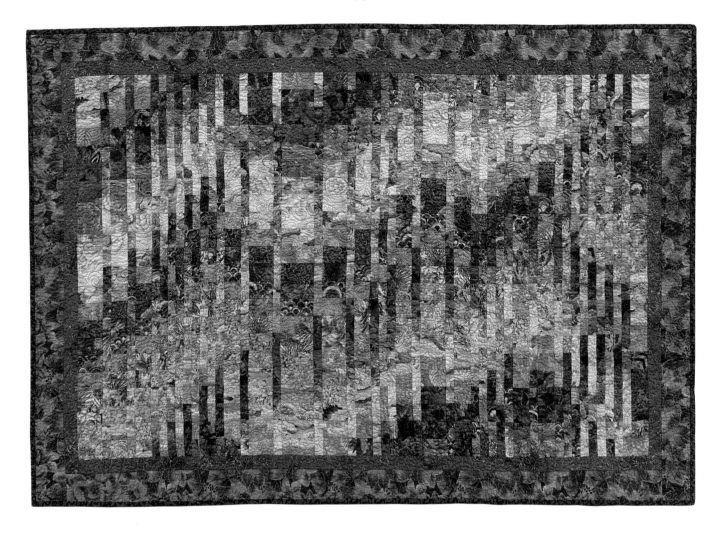

MIRAGE by Beth Ann Williams, 2000, Grand Rapids, Michigan, 56¾" x 39".

This bargello design features separator strips, which create secondary patterns of dancing color and light. This technique increases visual complexity with little increase in sewing difficulty. Care must be taken, however, when laying out the bargello segments; there are two active design lines to follow this time!

# MATERIALS   42"-wide fabric

¼ yd. *each* of 22 fabrics for bargello segments
⅜ yd. for inner border
1⅞ yds. for outer border
3 yds. for backing
½ yd. for binding
66¼" x 47½" piece of batting

# CUTTING

Cut strips on the crosswise grain (from selvage to selvage) unless otherwise stated. All measurements include ¼"-wide seam allowances.

**From *each* of the 22 bargello-segment fabrics, cut:**
2 strips, each 2" wide

**From the inner border fabric, cut:**
2 strips, each 1¾" wide, for inner side borders
3 strips, each 1¾" wide, for inner top and bottom borders

**From the outer border fabric, cut:**
2 strips on the lengthwise grain, each 4¼" wide, for outer side borders
2 strips on the lengthwise grain, each 4¼" wide, for outer top and bottom borders

**From the backing fabric, cut:**
2 pieces, each 42" x 49"

**From the binding fabric, cut:**
6 strips, each 2½" wide

# MAKING THE QUILT

You will need 2 identical strip sets for this quilt. One strip set will have its seam allowances pressed toward the first strip, and the other will have its seam allowances pressed toward the last strip.

1. Label and sew strip sets as described in "Sewing the Strip Sets" on page 32.

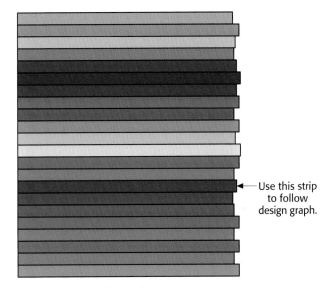

← Use this strip to follow design graph.

Make 2 identical strip sets.
Press seam allowances of first strip set toward top strip; press seam allowances of second strip set toward bottom strip.

2. With the first strip set, create a tube by sewing the unsewn edge of the first strip to the unsewn edge of the last strip. Sew with right sides together. Repeat for the second strip set. You should have 2 tubes.
3. Cut and label the bargello segments as described in "Cutting the Bargello Segments" on page 34. Use the widths listed in the following segment charts.

## ODD-NUMBERED BARGELLO SEGMENTS

Cut loops for odd-numbered segments from the first tube. The total width of loops cut from the first tube is 46½". All measurements include ¼"-wide seam allowances.

| Bargello segment number | Cut width |
|---|---|
| 1 | 2¾" |
| 3 | 2" |
| 5 | 2" |
| 7 | 1¼" |
| 9 | 1¼" |
| 11 | 1¼" |
| 13 | 1¼" |
| 15 | 2" |
| 17 | 2¾" |
| 19 | 3½" |
| 21 | 2¾" |
| 23 | 2" |
| 25 | 1¼" |
| 27 | 2" |
| 29 | 2¾" |
| 31 | 2" |
| 33 | 1¼" |
| 35 | 1¼" |
| 37 | 2" |
| 39 | 2" |
| 41 | 1¼"* |
| 43 | 1¼"* |
| 45 | 1¼"* |
| 47 | 1¼"* |
| 49 | 2"* |

*These segments can be cut from the other tube. However, be sure to press the seam allowances up instead of down.

## EVEN-NUMBERED BARGELLO SEGMENTS

Cut loops for even-numbered segments from the second tube. The total width of loops cut from the second tube is 30". All measurements include ¼"-wide seam allowances.

| Bargello segment number | Cut width |
|---|---|
| 2 | 1¼" |
| 4 | 1¼" |
| 6 | 1¼" |
| 8 | 1¼" |
| 10 | 1¼" |
| 12 | 1¼" |
| 14 | 1¼" |
| 16 | 1¼" |
| 18 | 1¼" |
| 20 | 1¼" |
| 22 | 1¼" |
| 24 | 1¼" |
| 26 | 1¼" |
| 28 | 1¼" |
| 30 | 1¼" |
| 32 | 1¼" |
| 34 | 1¼" |
| 36 | 1¼" |
| 38 | 1¼" |
| 40 | 1¼" |
| 42 | 1¼" |
| 44 | 1¼" |
| 46 | 1¼" |
| 48 | 1¼" |

4. Open the bargello loops as described in "Laying Out the Body of the Quilt" on page 35. Shift the dominant fabric up or down one segment each time, following the movement of the design graph on page 79.

5. Move the masking-tape labels to the top of each bargello segment. Referring to "Laying Out the Body of the Quilt," lay out the segments to check the flow of the design. Confirm that all seam allowances have been pressed in the correct direction so they will butt against each other when the segments are sewn together.

6. Sew the bargello segments together as described in "Assembling the Body of the Quilt" on page 36.

7. As described in "Adding Borders" on page 36, sew 2 inner border strips to the sides of the bargello section. Then sew the remaining 3 inner border strips together on the diagonal to yield 1 long strip. Cut this strip into 2 strips for

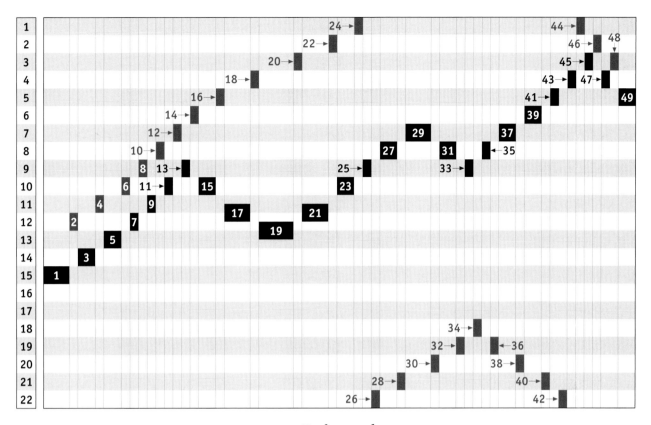

**Design graph**

the inner top and bottom borders; sew these pieces to the bargello section. Finally, sew the outer border strips to the quilt.

8. For the backing, sew the two 42" x 49" pieces together to yield one 83½" x 49" piece. Trim the backing so it is 2" to 4" larger all around than your quilt top. Layer and baste the quilt top, batting, and backing. Quilt as desired. See "Choosing a Quilting Method" on page 85 for tried-and-true suggestions for quilting bargello quilts.

9. Square up the quilt sandwich as described in "Squaring Up" on page 88.

10. If desired, sew a display sleeve to the back of your quilt. See "Adding a Sleeve" on page 89.

11. Sew on the binding. See "Binding" on page 91 for detailed instructions.

12. Sign and date your work, and enjoy your creation!

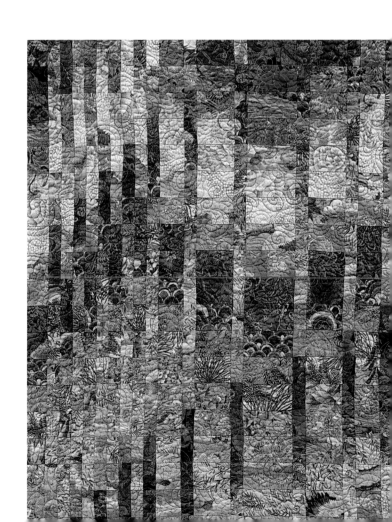

# ENCHANTED CARPET

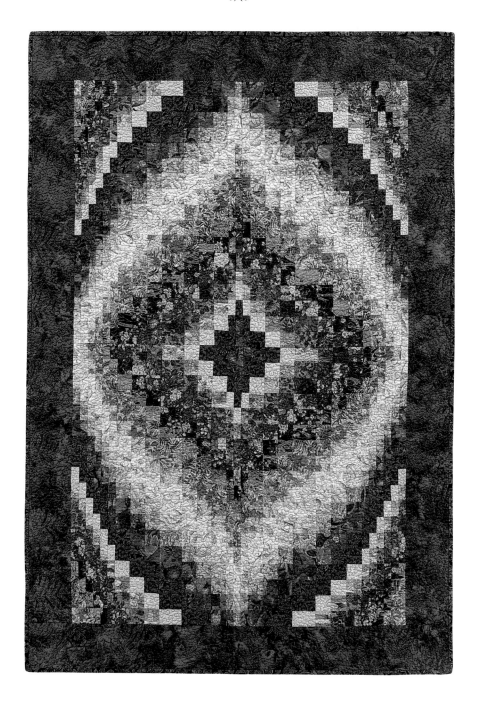

ENCHANTED CARPET by Beth Ann Williams, 2000, Grand Rapids, Michigan, 40¼" x 57½".

I am drawn to the slightly mysterious beauty of many intricate oriental carpets and kilims. Inspired by such pieces, this quilt retains some of the exotic flavor of the originals but is much easier to make! The two almost identical halves of the quilt are constructed separately and then joined together to form the completed medallion design.

# MATERIALS   42"-wide fabric

¼ yd. *each* of 18 fabrics for bargello segments (fat
    quarters are acceptable for this project)
1⅞ yds. for border
2⅞ yds. for backing
½ yd. for binding
46¾" x 65½" piece of batting

# CUTTING

Cut strips on the crosswise grain (from selvage to
selvage) unless otherwise stated. All measurements
include ¼"-wide seam allowances.

**From *each* of the 18 bargello-segment fabrics, cut:**
    6 strips, each 2" x 22"

**From the border fabric, cut:**
    2 strips on lengthwise grain, each 4¾" wide, for
        side borders*
    2 strips on lengthwise grain, each 4¾" wide, for
        top and bottom borders*

**From the backing fabric, cut:**
    2 pieces, each 42" x 46"

**From the binding fabric, cut:**
    6 strips, each 2½" wide

*You will adjust the length of the border strips after you
have completed the bargello section.

# MAKING THE QUILT

You will need 6 identical strip sets for this quilt.
Three strip sets you make will have their seam
allowances pressed toward the first strip, and the
second 3 will have their seam allowances pressed
toward the last strip.

If you have tried one of the other projects in this
book, notice that when you get to step 3, the
sequence for cutting loops from the 6 tubes varies
somewhat from the other projects. Also, notice that
steps 4 through 7 for preparing the segments and
assembling the quilt top vary from the instructions
for the other projects.

1. Label and sew strip sets as described in "Sewing
    the Strip Sets" on page 32. For this quilt, you will
    make 2 separate bargello panels that are almost
    identical. Then you will join them to make the
    completed bargello quilt top.

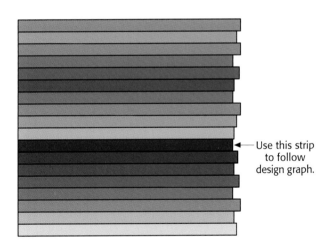

Use this strip
to follow
design graph.

Make 6 identical strip sets.
Press seam allowances of first 3 strip sets
toward top strip; press seam allowances
of second 3 strip sets toward bottom strip.

2. With the first strip set, create a tube by sewing
    the unsewn edge of the first strip to the unsewn
    edge of the last strip. Sew with right sides togeth-
    er. Repeat for the other 5 strip sets. You should
    have 6 tubes. Use low-tack masking tape to
    number the tubes 1 through 6.

## ODD-NUMBERED BARGELLO SEGMENTS

Cut one set of loops for odd-numbered segments from tube 4. Put these segments aside and cut a second set of odd-numbered segments from the remainder of tube 4 and from part of tube 5. The total width of one set of loops is 24¾". The total width of both sets is 49½". All measurements include ¼"-wide seam allowances.

| Bargello segment number | Cut width |
|---|---|
| 1 | 1¼" |
| 3 | 1¼" |
| 5 | 1¼" |
| 7 | 2" |
| 9 | 2" |
| 11 | 2" |
| 13 | 2" |
| 15 | 1¼" |
| 17 | 2" |
| 19 | 2" |
| 21 | 2" |
| 23 | 2" |
| 25 | 1¼" |
| 27 | 1¼" |
| 29 | 1¼" |

## EVEN-NUMBERED BARGELLO SEGMENTS

Cut one set of loops for even-numbered segments from tube 1. Put these segments aside and cut a second set of even-numbered segments from the remainder of tube 1 and from part of tube 2. The total width of one set of loops is 23½". The total width of both sets is 47". All measurements include ¼"-wide seam allowances.

| Bargello segment number | Cut width |
|---|---|
| 2 | 1¼" |
| 4 | 1¼" |
| 6 | 1¼" |
| 8 | 2" |
| 10 | 2¾" |
| 12 | 2" |
| 14 | 1¼" |
| 16 | 1¼" |
| 18 | 2" |
| 20 | 2¾" |
| 22 | 2" |
| 24 | 1¼" |
| 26 | 1¼" |
| 28 | 1¼" |

3. For the first bargello panel, cut and label the even-numbered bargello segments as described in "Cutting the Bargello Segments" on page 34. Use the widths listed in the even-numbered segment chart. Use tubes 1 and 2 (with seam allowances pressed up). Save what's left over from tube 2 to use later.

   Cut and label the odd-numbered bargello segments using the widths listed in the odd-numbered segment chart. Use tubes 4 and 5 (with seam allowances pressed down). Save what's left over from tube 5 to use later.

4. Open the bargello loops as described in "Laying Out the Body of the Quilt" on page 35. Shift the dominant fabric up or down one segment each time, following the movement of the design graph on page 83.

5. Referring to "Laying Out the Body of the Quilt," lay out the segments to check the flow of the design. Confirm that all seam allowances have been pressed in the correct direction so they will butt against each other when the segments are sewn together.

6. Sew the bargello segments together as described in "Assembling the Body of the Quilt" on page 36. You have now completed the first bargello panel.

7. To make the second bargello panel, use the widths from the even-numbered bargello segment chart to cut loops from tube 3 and the remainder of tube 2 (seam allowances pressed up). Use the widths from the odd-numbered bargello segment chart to cut loops from tube 6 and the leftovers of tube 5 (seam allowances pressed down).

8. Take care with this step! Just as you did in step 4, label the dominant fabric in each loop, open the bargello loops, and move the masking-tape labels to the top piece in each segment. As you open each loop, remove the last piece in the segment.

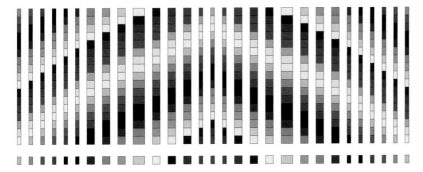

Second Bargello Panel
Remove the last piece from each segment.

9. Repeat steps 5 and 6 to lay out and sew the segments. You have now finished the second bargello panel.

10. To complete the bargello design, rotate the second panel and sew it to the first panel.

11. As described in "Adding Borders" on page 36, sew the side, top, and bottom border strips to the bargello section.

12. Sew the two 42" x 46" pieces together to make one 83½" x 46" piece. Trim the backing so it is 2" to 4" larger all around than your quilt top. Layer and baste the quilt top, batting, and backing. Quilt as desired. See "Choosing a Quilting Method" on page 85 for tried-and-true suggestions for quilting bargello quilts.

13. Square up the quilt sandwich as described in "Squaring Up" on page 88.

14. If desired, sew a display sleeve to the back of your quilt. See "Adding a Sleeve" on page 89.

15. Sew on the binding. See "Binding" on page 91 for detailed instructions.

16. Sign and date your work, and enjoy your creation!

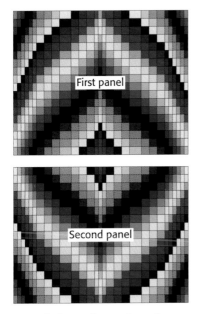

Join first and second panels.

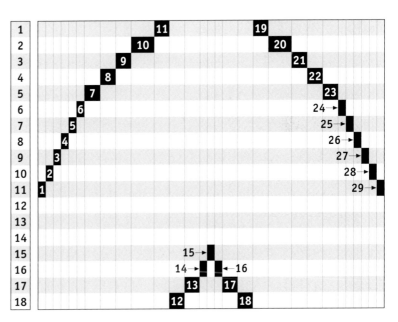

**Design graph**

# FINISHING TECHNIQUES

Once you have completed your bargello panel and added borders, you are ready to turn your project into a quilt. You will baste a quilt sandwich consisting of the bargello quilt top, batting, and backing. Then you will quilt the layers by hand or machine, square up the quilt, bind it, and block it. If your bargello quilt is destined to become a wall hanging, you may also want to add a sleeve to the back before you bind the quilt.

## BASTING THE QUILT SANDWICH

If you plan to machine quilt your project, pin basting is an easy and efficient way to baste the quilt sandwich. For medium-to-large wall hangings, lap quilts, or bed quilts that will be quilted by machine, I prefer to baste my quilt sandwich with safety pins, usually placing them approximately 3" apart.

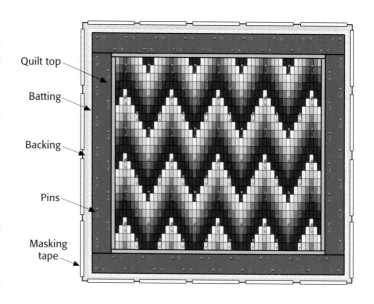

1. Press your quilt top and backing to remove any wrinkles.
2. Lay the backing wrong side up on a clean floor or table.
3. Use wide masking or packing tape (check first to make sure that the tape you are using will

84

not ruin the finish on your floor or table when you pull it up) to tape down all the edges, beginning with the centers of each side of the backing and then the corners. Then fill in around the entire perimeter of the quilt. The backing fabric should be smooth and taut, but not stretched so tightly that the fabric becomes distorted. If you stretch the fabric too much, it will spring back when you remove the tape and create a mess of wrinkles and tucks on the back side of your quilt.

> # TIP:
>
> As an alternative to tape, or if your quilt top is larger than your work area, you may also use clamps or binder clips to secure one or more edges of your backing fabric.
>
> **Tabletop** | **Backing (wrong side)**

4. Lay the batting on the backing, and smooth it in place. Remember that your backing and batting should be larger all around than your quilt top.
5. Smooth the quilt top into place.
6. Start pinning! Unlike many quilters, I like to pin the outer edges first so that the border seams stay straight and I don't disturb or distort them when I reach (or crawl) over them to pin the interior area of the quilt. However, if you are concerned that you might end up with a center bulge, you can start pinning in the center and work outward. Pin the interior of the quilt in grid fashion, with pins placed at 3" intervals.

Unless I need to crawl over some of the pins in order to reach other areas of the quilt, I like to wait until all the pins are in place before I close them.

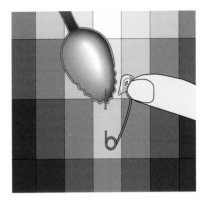

A grapefruit spoon is an effective tool for closing safety pins. The serrated edge helps keep the pin from slipping as you work.

# CHOOSING A QUILTING METHOD

Whether to quilt by hand or machine is strictly a matter of personal preference and aesthetic choice. Due to the small pieces and abundant seam allowances in a bargello quilt, I prefer quilting these projects by machine. However, it is possible to hand quilt a bargello quilt successfully!

## HAND QUILTING

Hand quilting a bargello project is easiest if the quilting lines are planned to avoid seam allowances as much as possible. For design ideas, see the section on "Machine-Guided (Walking Foot) Quilting" on page 86. Some of the same stitching patterns are easily adapted for hand quilting. When it comes to borders, you may wish to channel quilt, or you may opt to use a pretty stencil instead. For detailed information on hand-quilting techniques for both beginners and experts, see Roxanne McElroy's book *That Perfect Stitch* (The Quilt Digest Press, 1998) and Jeana Kimball's book *Loving Stitches: A Guide to Fine Hand Quilting* (That Patchwork Place, 1993).

## MACHINE QUILTING

### Hand-Guided (Free-Motion) Quilting

You'll notice that almost all of the quilts shown have been free-motion quilted. "Aurora" on page 68 and "Monet's Garden" on page 56 were quilted on a long-arm professional quilting machine by Terrie Wicks. I quilted all the other projects shown in this book on a home (non-industrial) sewing machine. I tend to free-motion quilt almost everything in sight, partly because I enjoy the process, and partly because I like to use the quilting as an additional design element. Dense quilting and decorative threads create subtle highlights and fabulous texture that both unifies the bargello—increasing the illusion of a single, unbroken, glowing surface—and adds visual complexity and interest.

Here are some of the free-motion patterns I use.

Free-Motion Quilting Designs

**To set up your machine for free-motion quilting:**

1. Attach a darning foot. (See "Sewing Machine and Attachments" on page 10.)
2. Lower the feed dogs. If you cannot lower your feed dogs, you may have a cover that snaps in place over them. I have found in my classes, however, that this cover often restricts movement of the darning foot. In those cases, it is best to leave the feed dogs alone and set the stitch length to 0. You might feel some additional drag on the fabric, but the darning foot should still allow the quilt to move freely.
3. Set the pressure on the presser foot to 0 (if applicable for your machine).
4. Make a sample quilt sandwich to test and adjust (if necessary) the tension settings. See "Tip" on page 87.
5. Away you go! Well, almost. Before you begin sewing, see the next section, "Securing the Stitch," on page 87.

### Machine-Guided (Walking Foot) Quilting

If you're not ready to jump full tilt into free-motion work, here are some suggestions for machine-guided quilting with a walking foot.

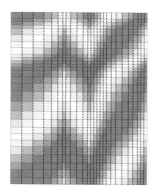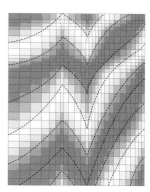

"In the ditch" along vertical seams

Following design lines

**Walking Foot Quilting Designs**

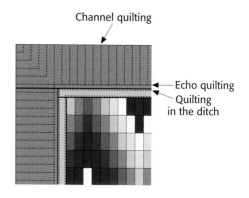

Channel quilting

Echo quilting
Quilting in the ditch

**To set up your machine for machine-guided quilting:**

1. Attach a walking foot. (See "Sewing Machine and Attachments" on page 10.)
2. Leave the feed dogs up (the same position they are in for normal sewing).
3. If possible, lower the pressure on the presser foot slightly. For example, if a normal pressure setting for your machine is 3, then try setting the dial back to 2, in order to decrease the drag on the presser foot.
4. Set the stitch length to about 10 stitches per inch (roughly the same setting as you would use for most piecing).
5. Make a sample quilt sandwich to test and adjust (if necessary) the tension settings.
6. Away you go! Well, almost. Before you begin sewing, see the next section, "Securing the Stitch," below.

---

TIP:

Depending on the combination of needle and thread(s) that you are using, it may be necessary to adjust the tension on the top thread to get a balanced stitch. If the top thread is showing on the back side of your work, increase the tension setting (turn it to a slightly higher number). If the bobbin thread is showing on the top side of your work, reduce the tension setting (turn it to a lower number).

---

## Securing the Stitch

The threads must be secured at the beginning and the end of every line of stitching. Securing the stitching may seem like a fussy step in making a quilt, but it's necessary.

1. With the top thread held above (not under) the presser foot, lower your presser foot.

2. Use the hand wheel on your machine to make one complete stitch, with the take-up lever starting in the highest position and stopping in the highest position.
3. Pull gently on the top thread, and the bobbin thread should pop up through all the layers.
4. Pull the end of the bobbin thread through so you can hold both threads under the presser foot and out of the way when you start stitching.
5. Continue holding both threads until you have locked your stitches; then you can relax. (If you don't pull the bobbin thread up, or don't hold onto both threads when you start stitching, you can end up with a nasty nest of thread on the back side of your work and/or have the bobbin thread sucked into the feed dogs, jamming the machine.) You can go back and clip the thread tails later.
6. While firmly holding (but not pulling) the top and bobbin threads, secure your stitches with a locking stitch—taking several stitches almost on top of each other—or by stitching about ¼" worth of tiny stitches (more than 20 stitches per inch).
7. At the end of a line of stitching, secure the stitches by using another locking stitch or by shortening your stitch length to more than 20 stitches per inch for the last ⅜" to ¼" of that line.

# TIPS ON QUILTING BY MACHINE

Here are a few things to remember to help you along while quilting by machine.

- Whatever style of quilting you do, it is important to distribute the quilting evenly across the quilt; if one area is quilted heavily and another is not, it is likely that your finished quilt will not lie flat.
- For either kind of machine quilting—unless you are starting on the outermost edge of the quilt so

the stitching will be enclosed under the binding—always be sure to bring up the bobbin thread through all layers at the beginning of a line of stitching. Hold both the top and bobbin threads until after the stitching has been secured; then clip them. (See "Securing the Stitch" at left.)

- For either kind of machine quilting, secure your threads not only at the beginning of every line of stitching but also at the end of every stitching line.
- When trimming threads at the end of a line of stitching, clip the top thread first as close as you can to the surface of the quilt; then turn the quilt over and tug on the bobbin thread to pull the "whisker" of top thread into the batting. Hold the bobbin thread taut, and clip it as close to the quilt as possible. When the thread relaxes, it too is drawn back into the batting.
- As you stitch, remember to look ahead to where you are going to quilt next, not at the needle. (This may take some practice to build confidence in your hand-eye coordination.)
- BREATHE!

## TROUBLESHOOTING

If you are experiencing difficulty with thread tension, or your thread and/or needle is breaking, check the following possibilities.

- Presser foot not lowered at start of sewing
- Thread ends not secured. (See "Securing the Stitch" on page 87)
- Thread caught on spool pin
- Thread tension improperly balanced. (See "Tips on Quilting by Machine" on page 87.)
- Lint buildup and/or bits of thread in the tension discs, around the presser bar and needle bar, under the needle plate, or especially in and around the bobbin area
- Needle inserted improperly
- Bent or dull needle
- Weight of quilt pulling against machine
- Too much fabric jammed up under machine (no room to maneuver)

# SQUARING UP

When you are finished with all the quilting, lay your project on your work surface (or clean floor). Does it lie flat? If not, consider adding a bit more quilting in any area that is rippling or puffing up. (A limited amount of fullness may also be tamed by blocking the quilt after you wash it.) Are the edges straight? Use your rotary ruler to make sure that the corners form a true 90° angle and that the quilt's edges are indeed straight. If they are not, you may need to "sliver trim" some edges with your rotary cutter.

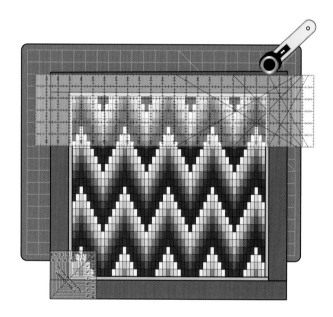

Slide your cutting mat under the quilt, positioning it beneath those areas that need to be straightened. Don't worry about cutting into quilting lines; all the lines of stitching will be secured when you attach the binding.

Measure the top and bottom of the quilt; the measurements should be equal. Do the same for the sides of the quilt.

# ADDING A SLEEVE

Most quilt shows require a 3" to 4" hanging sleeve; I also find that sleeves are handy for hanging pieces at home. My favorite display method is invisible from the front, with the quilt lying flush against the wall with no visible means of support.

## FORMAL SLEEVE

1. Cut the sleeve the same length as the measurement of the top edge of the quilt, and 7" to 9" wide (depending on whether you want a 3" or 4" finished sleeve).

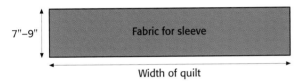

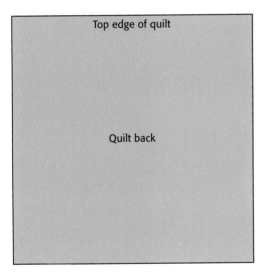

2. Fold the short edges under twice, about ⅜" each time, on the wrong side of the sleeve fabric; press. Topstitch the folds to form a finished edge.

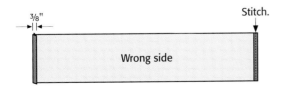

3. Fold the fabric in half lengthwise, right side out, and press. Pin the folded sleeve in place, matching raw edges of the sleeve with the top raw edge of the quilt sandwich. The quilt should extend approximately ¾" beyond the sleeve at either end.

4. Stitch the top edge of the sleeve in place, using a scant ¼"-wide seam allowance. This seam will be covered when you add the binding.

5. Hand stitch the other edge of the sleeve to the back of the quilt, making sure that your stitches do not show on the front of the quilt.

## EASY (NO HAND-SEWING) SLEEVE

1. Measure the width of the longest border at the top edge of the quilt. Double this measurement, and add ⅜" to determine the width of your sleeve.

2. Cut the sleeve to the same length as the measurement of the longest border at the top edge of the quilt. (This is generally the same length as the top edge of the quilt itself.)

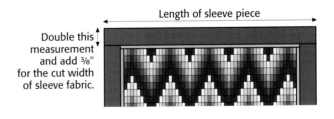

3. Fold the short edges under twice, about ⅜" each time, on the wrong side of the sleeve fabric; press. Topstitch the folds to form a finished edge, just as you would for a formal sleeve.

4. Center and pin this rectangle in place, wrong side up, on the back side of the quilt. One long edge should be even with the top edge of the quilt.

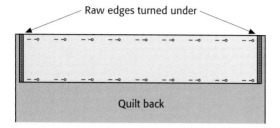

Raw edges turned under

Quilt back

5. With nylon monofilament thread in the top, and mercerized cotton thread to match your backing fabric in the bobbin, stitch from the front side of the quilt in the ditch along the longest border seam. Do not worry about crossing any of your quilting lines. This stitching will be hidden and will not interfere with other quilting lines, including free-motion work.

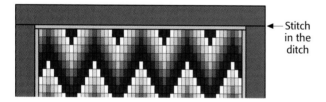

Stitch in the ditch

6. From the back side of the quilt, fold the rectangle in half so that both raw edges are even with the top edge of the quilt. (Because of the extra ⅜" added at the beginning, the fold will not line up perfectly with the stitching. This extra fullness in the sleeve helps to compensate for the width of a hanging rod.)

7. Pin and stitch the top edge of the sleeve in place, using a scant ¼"-wide seam allowance. This seam will be covered when you add the binding.

Slight fullness in sleeve

To hang a completed quilt at home, I take a 2½"- to 3"-wide wooden lattice or molding strip cut to the same length as the finished sleeve and add eyelet screws to either end. The eyelet screws hang on nails in my wall. To minimize wear and tear on the wall, I use the smallest nails capable of supporting the quilt's weight. The eyelet screws are completely hidden underneath the quilt, between the edge of the hanging sleeve and the binding.

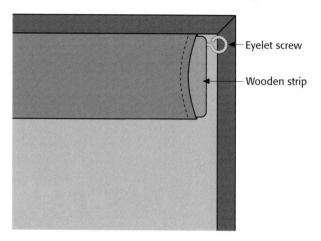

Eyelet screw

Wooden strip

TIP:

If you are using wooden lattice strips, molding, or dowels, be sure to seal the wood before putting it in contact with your quilt. This will protect the fabric from the acids in the wood. You can do this with varnish, paint, or even acrylic spray sealer.

# BINDING

I usually finish a quilt with a narrow double-fold binding, cut 2½" wide and finishing at ⅜" wide. Since the edges of these quilts are all straight, cut the binding fabric from selvage to selvage on the straight of grain, not on the bias.

## PREPARE THE BINDING

1. Join the binding strips with a diagonal seam.

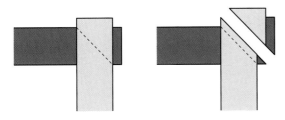

2. Press the seams open.
3. Fold the binding in half lengthwise with wrong sides together; then press.

Fold line

4. Open the binding strip at its starting end and fold the lower corner inward to create a 45° angle.
5. Leaving a ¼" seam allowance, trim away the tip of the triangle formed on the inside of the binding.

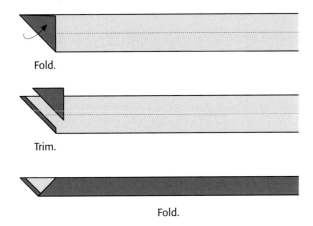

Fold.

Trim.

Fold.

6. Refold the binding strip.

## MACHINE SEW THE BINDING TO THE QUILT FRONT

1. Lay the binding around the quilt to make sure that the seams of the joined binding strips will not fall on the corners of the quilt.
2. When you are satisfied with the placement, position the beginning of the binding (the triangular edge) on the right side of the quilt, with the raw edges of the binding even with the raw edges of the quilt sandwich.
3. Leaving the first 5" unsewn, stitch the binding to the right side of the quilt with a ⅜"-wide seam allowance. Use a walking foot to keep the binding from becoming stretched or distorted while you sew.
4. Stop stitching ⅜" from the first corner.
5. With the needle down, pivot the quilt and stitch straight off the corner at a 45° angle.

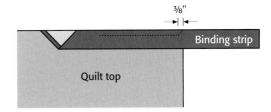

⅜"

Binding strip

Quilt top

6. Fold the binding strip up and away from the corner; then fold it back down and even with the next edge to create a pleat in the binding. Make sure the pleat is straight, and even with the edge of the quilt.

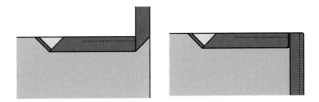

7. Holding the thread out of the way, slide the edge of the quilt back under your presser foot. Beginning right at the edge of the quilt, resume normal sewing.
8. Continue in the same manner around the remaining edges and corners.

9. Stop sewing several inches away from the starting point. Stop with the needle down, and keep the presser foot down as well.

10. Open the fold you made at the beginning of the binding, and tuck the end of the binding inside to determine how much excess length can be trimmed away.

11. Cut the extra fabric away, making sure that the beginning and ending of the binding overlap each other about 1".

12. Tuck the end back inside the fold so that no cut edges are exposed.

13. Sew through all layers, overlapping where you started stitching the binding at the beginning.

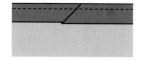

14. Turn the folded edge of the binding over the raw edge of the quilt and hand stitch it in place. The binding on the back of the quilt should cover the previous line of machine stitching that attaches the binding to the quilt top.

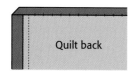
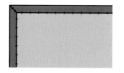

As you hand stitch the binding in place on the back of the quilt, make sure that your stitches do not go through all the layers; you do not want them to show on the front of the quilt.

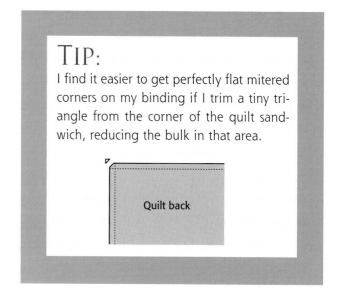

TIP:
I find it easier to get perfectly flat mitered corners on my binding if I trim a tiny triangle from the corner of the quilt sandwich, reducing the bulk in that area.

Quilt back

15. As you come to the corners, stitch down the binding miters on both the front and back of the quilt.

16. Stitch down the tucked end of the binding.

# WASHING AND BLOCKING

The first thing I do when I complete a quilt is wash it. Washing removes any stiffness, as well as dust, cat hair, and other "foreign matter." It also allows the stitching to sink into the batting, creating a softer finished look. A quilt that has been machine quilted with nylon monofilament thread, in particular, looks much better after it has been washed. Methods for washing and drying quilts can be somewhat controversial, so use the method that works best for you! Here are the washing steps that I take for non-antique quilts.

1. Wash quilt in the washer, in warm water, on the gentle cycle. Synthrapol or Orvus quilt soap are my favorite products for laundering my quilts.

2. Dry the quilt in the dryer on a gentle setting; if possible, take it out when it is still slightly damp.

3. Lay the quilt out to finish drying on a clean cotton blanket or mattress pad, making sure the quilt is perfectly flat and the edges perfectly straight. If necessary, while it is drying, lightly steam-press and block any area that is uncooperative. The edges should be straight, the corners square, and quilted areas free from distortion.

4. Allow the blocked quilt to cool and dry completely before disturbing it.

## TIPS:

• Try not to fold quilts that have been quilted very heavily. When possible, store them flat, layered (if necessary), on an extra guest bed. You can hang them on the wall or roll them, right side out, on large tubes that have been covered with muslin.

• Don't forget to air and rotate your quilts periodically, whether they are stored flat, rolled, or hung. These precautions can reduce strain on decorative stitching and prevent permanent fold lines from marring your quilts.

# SIGNING AND LABELING YOUR FINISHED PROJECT

Sign and date your work! You can write directly on the front and/or back of the quilt with a permanent, nonfading, waterproof ink. You can also attach a permanent label to the back of your quilt. Consider including at least the following information: title of quilt (if applicable), name of quiltmaker, name of designer (if other than quiltmaker), where quilt was made, and date quilt was made. Additional information may include the inspiration behind the quilt, the special significance of the quilt, or the person for whom the quilt was made. Posterity will thank you!

# BIBLIOGRAPHY AND SUGGESTED READING

Amsden, Deirdre. *Colourwash Quilts: A Personal Approach to Design and Technique*. Bothell, Wash.: That Patchwork Place, Inc., 1994.

Barnes, Charles, and David P. Blake. *Bargello and Related Stitchery*. Great Neck, N.Y.: Hearthside Press, Inc., 1971.

Barnes, Christine. *Color: The Quilter's Guide*. Bothell, Wash.: That Patchwork Place, Inc., 1997.

Doheny, Marilyn. *Bargello Tapestry Quilting*. Edmonds, Wash.: Doheny Publications, 1993.

Edie, Marge. *Bargello Quilts*. Bothell, Wash.: That Patchwork Place, Inc., 1994.

Itten, Johannes. *The Art of Color*. New York: Van Nostrand Reinhold, 1973.

Johannah, Barbara. *Barbara Johannah's Crystal Piecing*. Radnor, Pa.: Chilton Book Company, 1993.

Noble, Maurine. *Machine Quilting Made Easy*. Bothell, Wash.: That Patchwork Place, 1994.

Penders, Mary Coyne. *Color and Cloth: The Quiltmaker's Ultimate Workbook*. San Francisco, Calif.: The Quilt Digest Press, 1989.

Magaret, Pat Maixner, and Donna Ingram Slusser. *Watercolor Quilts*. Bothell, Wash.: That Patchwork Place, 1994.

———. *Watercolor Impressions*. Bothell, Wash.: That Patchwork Place, 1995.

Spingola, Deanna. *Strip-Pieced Watercolor Magic*. Bothell, Wash.: That Patchwork Place, 1996.

McElroy, Roxanne. *That Perfect Stitch: The Secrets of Fine Hand Quilting*. San Francisco, Calif.: The Quilt Digest Press, 1998.

Williams, Elsa S. *Bargello, Florentine Canvas Work*. New York: Van Nostrand Reinhold Company, 1967.

Wold, Diane. *Strip Quilting*. Blue Ridge Summit, Pa.: TAB Books, 1987.

Wolfrom, Joen. *The Magical Effects of Color*. Martinez, Calif.: C&T Publishing, 1992.

# RESOURCES

I purchased some of my supplies from the following companies:

**Connecting Threads**
PO Box 8940
Vancouver, WA 98668-8940
Phone: (800) 574-6454
Fax: (360) 260-8877
Web Site: www.ConnectingThreads.com
*Free catalog available upon request.*

**Clotilde**
B3000
Louisiana, MO 63353-3000
Phone: (800) 772-2891
or outside the USA, (573) 754-7979
Fax: (800) 863-3191 or (573) 754-3109
Web Site: www.clotilde.com
*Free catalog available upon request.*

**Grand Quilt Co.**
5290 Alpine Avenue NW
Comstock Park, MI 49321
Phone: (616) 647-1120
Fax: (616) 647-1074
E-Mail: GrQuiltCo@aol.com
Web Site: www.grandquilt.com

**Hancock's of Paducah**
3841 Hinkleville Road
Paducah, KY 42001
Phone: (800) 845-8723
Web Site: www.Hancocks-Paducah.com
*Free catalog available upon request.*

**Nancy's Notions**
PO Box 683
Beaver Dam, WI 53916-0683
Phone: (800) 833-0690
Fax: (800) 255-8119
Web Site: www.nancysnotions.com
*Free catalog available upon request.*

Additional supplies were provided by:

**Hobbs Bonded Fibers**
200 South Commerce Drive
Waco, TX 76710
Phone: (254) 741-0040

**Superior Threads, Inc.**
PO Box 1672
St. George, UT 84771
Phone: (435) 652-1867

**YLI Corporation**
161 West Main Street
Rock Hill, SC 29730
Phone: (800) 296-8139
Fax: (803) 985-3106
Web Site: www.ylicorp.com

# ABOUT THE AUTHOR

Photo by Amy Logsdon

Although born in the United States, Beth Ann Williams has spent a significant portion of her life living and traveling overseas. As a result, she has enjoyed a lifelong fascination with the richness of varied cultural and artistic traditions. As a fourth-generation quiltmaker (at least!), Beth has a profound respect for traditional approaches to quiltmaking. However, she is best known for her contemporary quilts and innovative methods. Her award-winning work has appeared in galleries, museums, books, magazines, and in a calendar published by Martingale & Company. Individual pieces are included in both public and private collections.

Beth exhibits, lectures, and teaches workshops and classes on the regional and national levels, as well as locally at Grand Quilt Company in Comstock Park, Michigan. In addition to bargello techniques, she teaches in a variety of other subject areas, including Celtic quilt design, decorative machine quilting, heirloom machine appliqué, impressionist-style piecing, abstract design, and color theory.

Beth holds a B.A. in communication arts from Cedarville College, Cedarville, Ohio. She is a member of the West Michigan Quilter's Guild, the National Quilting Association, the American Quilter's Society, the American Quilt Study Group, and the International Quilt Association. This is Beth's second book with Martingale & Company; *Celtic Quilts: A New Look for Ancient Designs* was her first.